Poo, Power and Politics

Bob Able

Copyright © 2024 Bob Able

All rights reserved

The characters and events portrayed in this book are fictitious. Any similarity to real persons, living or dead, is coincidental and not intended by the author.

No part of this book may be reproduced, or stored in a retrieval system, or transmitted in any form or by any means, electronic, mechanical, photocopying, recording, or otherwise, without express written permission of the publisher.

==

"Although it might appear that way now, these people are not all crooks or buffoons. Mostly they mean well, at least to start with. But if you give a few bad apples power and influence, you cannot expect the sweetest cider.
Still, we can always vote them out next time, can't we?"

==

POO, POWER AND POLITICS

An amusing yet plausible tale of effluent, electricity and education; and dastardly political manoeuvres.

By Bob Able

INTRODUCTION:

Those mysterious Civil Servants who bustle like wavelets on the calm of London's Whitehall, doing whatever it is they do all day are mostly, as the expression goes "kept in the dark and occasionally covered in ….". Well, you get the idea.
But that is not always the case. Very rarely, under the right conditions, they have been known to rise up and take matters into their own hands.

Sometimes that is a good thing. Sometimes not. But there are occasions when a sharp and timely yank on the handbrake is just what is needed to keep their political masters on the straight and narrow.

And sometimes these mushrooms can be induced to tweak that handbrake so subtly that nobody, not even the Whitehall rats, ever guess they have been there.

ONE

… The action begins on a date in the not too distant future …

Tim Blande, with an 'e', had quite a good job.

He lived in quite a nice semi-detached house, in a quiet area. It had a quite small, but nevertheless secluded garden, and it was on a corner plot at the end of a quiet road. He was mostly quite content to live a quiet life.

Hazel Trigg was always called 'Twig' or 'Twiglet' at school and hated it.

She had underlined the 'r' in her name as a matter of course on the front of all her school books, and during that period of wild rebellion that takes us all in our last year at school, had referred to herself as tRigg, with a capital 'R' to try to dispel the confusion.

That didn't last, of course. But much to her irritation, her first 'business cards' when she started as a trainee journalist with the New Malden and Worcester Park Informer had to be sent back and reprinted when they announced her name as 'Twig', this time without even the saving grace of two 'g's'.

Now, some years later, she worked for 'The Gazette' and stalked the halls of Whitehall hoping to expose the next big scandal, for which that august monthly magazine was so well renowned.

That was where she met Tim Blande, with an 'e'.

To be precise, they actually met in a coffee shop which sold sandwiches at lunchtime to the office workers, and not being one of the more popular or trendy places, tended to have shorter queues and less aspirational prices.

Tim and Hazel had been in the same queue many times before, but it was not until Hazel tripped and launched her over-stuffed egg mayonnaise and tomato baguette into Tim's shirt front that they had a conversation.

Tim had always been reticent to push himself forward and endeavoured not to draw attention to himself in public places. He was also somewhat pernickety about his modestly priced but quietly businesslike work clothes, and kept an old-fashioned stiff brush, that had belonged to his father, in the top right-hand drawer of his desk.

Every lunchtime he plied the brush before venturing out to the sandwich shop, straightened his tie in the mirror in the lift, and gave each of his shoes a swift buff up on the backs of his trousers before leaving the building.

It was unfortunate that the weather was warm and he did not need to wear his raincoat, because the flying baguette caught the front of his clean white shirt, which was only on its second outing since it had been bought new from Marks & Spencer.

Hazel was mortified. The mess was bad enough, but it was the end of the month, and she was not sure she could afford another baguette to replace the one now dripping from the shirt of the dapper little man in front of her.

Both speaking at once, they said 'sorry' of course, and Hazel made a play of gathering up paper napkins and doing her best to mop up the mess. Until, that was, she was thrust aside by a bustling shop assistant with one of those peculiar floppy dustpans that lay flat to the floor at the end of a long handle, who started sweeping up with a rather threadbare broom.

Tim looked down in dismay at the front of his new shirt. It would be egg and tomato, wouldn't it? he thought.

But as he was looking down his eye met that of Hazel, coming up.

'Look, I'm most frightfully sorry,' she was saying. 'If I give you my business card, could you send me the dry-cleaning bill …'

'Oh no, it is quite all right,' said Tim automatically. 'I'm quite sure there is no harm done. No need to worry.'

But Hazel was pressing her business card into his hand and saying something about egg yolk stains when the tutting shop assistant finished sweeping up, and after giving them both a look that could melt broken glass, departed.

They both saw the unnecessarily fierce look, glanced at each other and found that they were laughing.

It was the start of a sometimes strained, but always interesting friendship.

-ooo0oo-

Tim worked for the Department for Water Supply and Sanitation, which doesn't sound terribly glamorous, but without which, as the Minister herself repeatedly stated, we would all drown in our own sewage.

Tim had started at the bottom, so to speak, in the department responsible for national foul drainage infrastructure, and worked his way up. Now in the same building but three floors up, he was one of several quite senior Civil Servants who had direct access to the Minister and would be expected to brief her on any new developments or emergencies as they arose.

If they arose, that was. Nothing too startling happened in the office managing Domestic Sanitation Standards where Tim was based, which, if you think about it, was probably just as well.

-ooOoo-

Amanda Trunnion MP, Tim's ultimate boss, was the relatively junior Minister in charge of the department and was a bluff, bombastic, self-important career politician.

She had been with her County Council for several years and eventually became Leader. The officers and Councillors there no doubt drew a collective sigh of relief when she stood for Parliament and was elected to the relatively safe seat she now represented in the Conservative interest.

Since her elevation to the role she now held, and with a minor, but as she insisted, important Ministerial post, she became even more puffed-up and difficult, and was prone to making silly errors which her Civil Servants continually had to clean up.

Most of her problems were of her own making and revolved around the fact that she did not 'do detail'. She would read 'executive summaries' and the first few lines of papers and letters and assume that was all she needed to do to understand the issues, sometimes with disastrous results.

The latest 'close thing' was caught just in time by a quite junior officer on her staff.

After some energetic lobbying she had at last worn down the Cabinet Minister she reported to, and by extension the PM, into allowing her department to set up a 'Commission'.

It was the ambition of most junior ministers to get their office a 'Commission' and publish results that would push on their careers. She, like most of those before her, had little interest in the subject matter, or the outcome, just the opportunity for career advancement.

Amanda, who was never a candidate to be a 'Mandy,' even at school, had persuaded her superiors to create a "Commission" looking into the state of rural drainage infrastructure, and in particular the potential for damage from sewerage and fertiliser run off into the rivers.

It was a serious project, and her first job was to come up with a name for the Commission and appoint experts to manage it.

She called together her Civil Servants and told them she proposed to call her project the 'Rural Run-off and Public Infrastructure Environmental Study.' That was fine until that junior officer pointed out that when you added the 'C' of 'Commission' to the front of it, and converted it to the inevitable acronym so beloved of Whitehall departments, you came up with 'CRRAPIES', so it had to be hastily re-named the Rural Infrastructure Environmental Commission, or 'RIEC' for short.

Tim Blande was seconded to work on the project under Patrick Blenny, who was not renowned for doing anything by way of actual work within the department where they were both employed. Tim became Patrick's deputy, which in reality meant he got to do all the work, while Patrick got the glory.

The appointment of 'experts and consultants' to the Commission was the next contentious issue.

Ms. Trunnion proposed to appoint Giles Norton-Bunkerman to head the Commission. He was an old friend of her family and farmed on the Shropshire borders.

The Civil Servant tasked with doing the background checks, before the appointment was made, had to report that the Norton-Bunkerman family had a large shareholding in an American chemical fertiliser company whose principal products were banned in Europe. In addition, it emerged that various family members had a highly visible presence at pro-hunting rallies, and had maintained a sizeable pack of hounds long after the hunting ban came into force.

He also had to report that Giles Norton-Bunkerman himself had recently had some miles of hedgerows removed on his farms, and had converted parts of his arable business to 'prairie farming' following an American 'mono-culture' model.

If that were not bad enough, it emerged that Giles Norton-Bunkerman had a business partner who was recently taken to court and fined for releasing raw creosote into ponds and rivers adjacent to his factory, which made garden sheds and fence panels. Furthermore, Giles himself was on record as having paid the fine.

When Ms. Trunnion proposed him for the role of Chairman, she had just returned from a shooting party on his estate. This, she explained without a glimmer of recognition of her situation, she had thoroughly enjoyed, and they had bagged the best haul of pheasants she could remember.

The senior Minister to whom she reported took her to one side and enlightened her on that one, and Ms. Trunnion was 'encouraged' to seek another nominee for the role of Chairman of her Commission.

Twice married and once widowed Ms. Trunnion was quick to propose her first ex-husband's brother for the role.

Sir Jacob Mortimer was a merchant banker, had made substantial donations to the party at the time of Ms. Trunnion's election, and was a familiar sight around the dining rooms of Westminster. He was accepted without a murmur from the Civil Servants on the instruction of the senior Minister.

Professor Edwin Potts was swiftly appointed as Chief Environmental Advisor to reprise a similar role he held for the previous Government. He was considered a safe pair of hands.

He helped in the selection of experts for the lesser advisory roles from the scientific community and would be working alongside Bethany Ford from the National Farmers Union and Sir Barton Parish, the head of the Highways Agency in England.

There were also roles for Philip Knowles from the Environment Agency, and slightly controversially, Piers Aubin from a company called Media Management & Promotions, to handle communications.

Aubin was a high-profile television and press promotor who had worked to create advertising and media opportunities and visibility for several footballers, a well-known plastic window company, and an up-and-coming professional golfer. He was also the chairman of a company that hired out carpet cleaning machines, and a director of a company selling 'funeral plans'.

After some initial meetings and the creation of a 'Protocol' for the Commission to work to, Tim Blande and Patrick Blenny organised and attended the first public meeting of all these appointees. It took place on a wet Wednesday morning in the Conference Room on the ground floor of the building next to their own offices in Whitehall.

A press release was issued, and various invited members of the media attended the event, including Hazel Trigg, representing 'The Gazette'.

-oo0Ooo-

'Hello Tim,' said Hazel shaking out her umbrella on the doorstep as Tim held the door open for her. 'Bit of a downpour.'

When they met in the coffee shop, over the weeks since the baguette incident, there had been smiles and little waves followed by greetings, and then polite comments about the weather. But the breakthrough came during a different sudden downpour.

On this occasion the sudden heavy rain effectively trapped the customers temporarily in the coffee shop and Hazel grabbed a chair by one of the little 'bistro tables' just inside the door and invited Tim to join her.

Their discussion then had been light and inevitably centred on the weather, and Hazel revealed that she worked from 'home' in the form of a little rented flat round the corner, so did not have too far to go when the rain stopped.

'My office is only just round the corner too, as it happens,' Tim offered. 'But I think a few minutes sheltering here is only sensible in this weather.'

'Rain was forecast, but I thought they said light showers on the news this morning, not this tropical storm!' smiled Hazel.

'It has been a bit unpredictable for a week or more now,' nodded Tim, and with the weather as their icebreaker, their conversation flowed quite comfortably as they decided to eat their sandwiches on the premises rather than risk a dash outside.

There were no actual 'dates' as such, but eating their sandwiches together in the coffee shop became quite a regular thing, and Tim found himself hoping it would rain at lunchtime to give them an excuse to do it again.

Hazel revealed that her 'official' office was just behind Canary Wharf, but that with her little flat in a more convenient location to be close to 'where the action is,' she rarely went there.

'Nowadays it is so easy to communicate using computers and the internet or mobile phones, I don't see that we need to go to offices at all anymore,' she said breezily.

'It will be a few lifetimes before my employers cotton on to that,' said Tim, and told Hazel a little of what his working environment was like, and his commute to work.

On another occasion Hazel revealed that she would love to live away from London.

'No chance of me being able to buy a place of my own, of course.

The rent on my flat gobbles up my salary and saving anything is almost impossible. When I want to see a bit of green and some grass and what-not, I have to be content with a walk in the park.'

The inevitable annual round of train strikes presented Tim with the next opportunity to spend a little more time with Hazel. The news was full of it, and Tim learned that his commute home would be disrupted with all the trains delayed for at least an hour, if they ran at all. In the coffee shop Hazel suggested that if he was interested, she could show him the park where she walked sometimes, to kill a little time before his train went that evening.

They did it again the next day, with Hazel helpfully getting 'live updates' on her mobile phone so that Tim could get to the station in good time for when the train did finally turn up.

On the third day, Tim found it very difficult to get to work, and there was no certainty that any trains would run at all. In the end, he endured a tortuous bus journey in to work, and worried that he would not be able to get home, he linked up with a group of his co-workers to 'block book' a series of hotel rooms in the Premier Inn just over the river. They were lucky to secure the rooms, and had it not been for the foresight of one of his colleagues to suggest booking eight or nine rooms at once, Tim thought they were unlikely to have been able to secure accommodation at all.

That night Hazel and Tim had dinner together in a little Greek place she knew just round the corner.

-oo0Ooo-

The press conference went off largely without incident, apart from when Patrick Blenny announced that Amanda Trunnion MP would speak next, and she nearly knocked the podium flying when she blundered onto the raised stage.

As the invited guests, media people, and other hangers-on were leaving, Hazel caught Tim's eye across the room and was soon at his side.

'That was interesting,' she said. 'Amanda Trunnion's speech was quite enlightening; I wonder if I could get a copy of it? I suppose someone else wrote it for her, of course. You don't happen to know who that was do you, Tim?'

Tim made a little noise in the back of his throat and felt suddenly quite hot. When Patrick Blenny asked him to do it, he had done his best to get the salient points across in the speech using simple language that Ms. Trunnion would not stumble over, and although it was fairly obvious that she had not actually read the speech all the way through until just before the event, he thought it had been OK.

'Erm, I'm sure I can get you a transcript, if you're interested, Hazel,' he said. 'Can I give you a printed copy at lunchtime in the coffee shop?'

-ooOoo-

Hazel read the speech again, sitting uncomfortably on her sofa bed that night. On the last page of the photocopy Tim handed her, right at the bottom in very small type, Hazel noticed some sort of a reference number, with the name T. Blande and the date at the end.

He had not admitted it, or been boastful about it as some men would, but Hazel now realised that Tim had written the speech, and although until now she had only called him by his first name, now she had his surname.

The internet is a wonderful resource if you know how to use it, and having trained as a journalist, Hazel knew how to look into all sorts of its corners and follow twists and turns to get what she wanted.

She soon had quite a lot of information about Timothy James

Blande including where he worked, where he went to school and university, and the fact that he had been married for over twenty years.

Whilst Hazel had to admit to herself that theirs was hardly a romance in the truest sense of the word, she had rather hoped that her friendship with Tim stood a chance of blossoming into something more.

Hazel did not go to the sandwich shop the next day.

-ooOoo-

TWO

P ressure is down a bit, but all the inward flows are good,' reported Ewan when his boss passed by and asked for an update.

'Right-ho,' nodded Dai, and continued on his way.

The control centre was much bigger than it needed to be, but was a good example of re-purposing on the site of the Second World War air-strip and camp. The fortified concrete building Ewan now regarded as his personal domain was easily and economically converted to its present use when the new facilities were built.

The site had seen many changes over the years, and now the concrete runway was almost entirely gone. It was replaced by the vast tanks and snaking pipework of the combined sewage treatment works, the field of solar panels, and the shining, newish, silver high-tech waste-to-energy digesters.

The control centre stood a little away from these massive structures, with one of the RAF's still sturdy concrete roads providing vehicular access.

The view from the small windows, cut into the side of the structure to provide some natural light and fresh air, was over the side of the plateau on which the airstrip was built. They looked past a few more ramshackle wartime buildings and down the slope towards a former coal mine, still with its tall towers in place, but now minus the iconic wheel.

In-between, sheep grazed on the lush grass which was dotted with patches of wild mushrooms. The huge pipeline, on high metal stilts, which fed the facility with effluent waste from several nearby urban conurbations, crossed the picturesque stream just down the slope.

In the distance a little wood and an outcrop of rock marked the edge of a former quarry, now converted into a caravan site and popular with holidaymakers, who benefitted from a steepish path which led down to the sea, and a nice sandy beach.

Ewan found the view peaceful and relaxing and with little sound from the facility itself, most of the time, unless the pumps were being back-flushed, it was a pleasant enough place to work. Certainly, Ewan thought, much better than the old deep mine down the hill where his father had spent his working life. Progress was not such a bad thing at all, he felt.

Dai, on his way back from his regular circuit of the facility glanced at the dials on Ewan's console.

'The pressure is right down, Ewan, look you. Another example of the methane levels dropping in the pipe mid-week. But you wait till all those townies have their curries on Friday night, then it will shoot right up again!'

The pair laughed at the oft-repeated jokes about how the eating habits of their 'customers', far away in the towns, affected what came down the pipe and Ewan returned to the crossword in his newspaper as Dai walked to the little office area behind flimsy dividers on the other side of the control centre building.

-ooOoo-

The problem, Patrick Blenny explained, was that although the visit to the hi-tech facility in Wales had been in the diary for months, Ms. Trunnion was not keen, and did not seem to want to engage in the arrangements for the event.

'She asked if we could find some way to make it relevant to the work of the Commission, and said that she wasn't interested in singing the praises of a project created under the last Labour administration.' Tim nodded; he had expected as much. 'So could you have a look at it and chat up the environment people to see if you can find something we can use to associate the two projects please Tim.'

Tim groaned inwardly. It would be difficult to make some useful connection between a project that pumped sewage, albeit treated sewage, into the sea, and a commission to look into managing and avoiding just that sort of run-off.

'The Cabinet has made it clear that we are not looking to denigrate the Welsh project, especially as it is likely to be replicated under the current administration in England as well, so we have to be careful,' added Patrick. 'There might be a cheap political point to be made if there was some problem with what it chucks out into the sea perhaps, but at the moment it is considered 'best practice' and there is nothing better to replace it, so the Government want to be seen to be supporting it.'

Tim looked at his watch. It was time for his trip to the sandwich shop. He hoped Hazel was going to be there this time, it had been three days since he had last seen her.

He wondered if Hazel knew about the Minister's visit to the Welsh facility, and if she proposed to attend.

-oooOoo-

There wasn't anything in the fridge, so there was nothing for it.

Today she would have to go to the sandwich shop for her lunch.

She was being silly, really, Hazel told herself. It was not as if they had dated or anything like that. So what if he was married, who wasn't these days?

She wasn't married, of course. The opportunity had never seemed to arise. She had had boyfriends, naturally. Strings of them, but nothing really serious.

Unless, of course, she went right back and allowed herself to remember Sammy from school.

It might have been love with Sammy, and it might have lasted if that blasted Susan Billings hadn't stuck her pneumatic chest in, and tempted him away.

Her romance with Sammy was a gentle, special, slow burning thing. Holding hands, and walks in the woods. Watercress tea at that old mill, and when he passed his test, drives out into the country and long dreamy kissing sessions under the stars, listening to The Carpenters on his car cassette player.

Hazel felt special and appreciated. Until she found out that the back seat of Sammy's old car was getting a workout with the bulbous Susan as well.

There had been others at university, of course.

Mind you, she had a lucky escape from Greg.

For some unfathomable reason she spent a full year thinking this was it, as serious, sober, academic Greg let her have his opinions on everything under the sun. Each date was more like attending a lecture, as she listened to his admittedly well read, but very opinionated views on politics, the emerging cult of personality, and the flagging prosperity of the nation.

Her note to end it, pinned to his front door, was succinct and to the point and she smiled at the memory of it now.

"Greg: You are, without question, the most irredeemably boring person I have ever met, or ever want to meet. Goodbye. Hazel."

Her friends told her that he didn't even seem to break step, and attached himself to a younger student almost instantly. She was well out of that.

As she pulled on her coat and checked that she had her purse and keys, she wondered what she would say to Tim, if he was there.

He might not even turn up of course, but she found that she was rather hoping he would.

-ooOoo-

Piers Aubin bustled up to the front desk.

'Piers Aubin, Media Management and Promotions,' he announced. 'Here for a meeting with The Minister.'

'Which Minister, sir?' said the unsmiling middle-aged woman behind the glass screen, who had seen it all before. 'We have several.'

'Amanda Trunnion,' blustered Piers, 'and I'm late.'

'If you would just like to step up to the security desk over to your left sir, for the bag check and to answer a few questions, you will soon be on your way.'

'Suck back!' exclaimed Piers. 'Do I have to go through all this ruddy rigmarole on every occasion I come here? It is very time consuming and inconvenient.'

'I'm afraid so sir. The security protocols must be followed, and we can't make any exceptions.'

Over his right shoulder, out of the corner of his eye, Piers thought he caught sight of Sir Jacob Mortimer coming through a side door surrounded by a blizzard of flunkies. They were waved past the security desk and disappeared into the inner lobby where there were lifts.

It occurred to Piers that Sir Jacob was probably on his way to the same meeting he was here to attend, but realising the inevitability of the process, he handed over his bag to be searched, and began to fill in the two-page form the security guard handed him.

-ooOOoo-

Professor Edwin Potts knew what to expect and arrived early for the meeting. He sat alone in the meeting room awaiting events.

As Chief Environmental Advisor to the Commission he commanded some respect in the corridors of Whitehall, and Philip Knowles from the Environment Agency treated him with particular deference.

The professor was unaware of the flattery he received, or perhaps was immune to it, and was modest and quiet in these meetings. But for those who did not know him, if a passion burned in his breast, he would show no outward sign of it. The outspoken Bethany Ford of the National Farmers Union had whispered to Sir Barton Parish, the head of the Highways Agency, that she thought the old boy was half asleep. Luckily Sir Barton was rather deaf so missed the disrespectful comment altogether.

Patrick Blenny called the meeting to order just as Piers Aubin, flustered and over-hot from rushing up the stairs, burst through the door.

Tim had been rushing too, but only to coax his little grey cells to come up with something, anything, that could align the Welsh project with the aims of the Commission. He considered what he had settled on was thin, and hoped it would not be too transparent to the audience Ms. Trunnion had now called together in the form of the selected members of the Commission.

-oo0Ooo-

'So,' said Tim as he and Hazel unwrapped their sandwiches in the coffee shop, 'what she wants to do is combine this long-planned trip to the Welsh facility with a 'fact finding mission for the Commission' and take some of the Committee along. She also proposes meeting a selection of journalists down there when she does her tour of the facilities'.

'So, she is turning it into a photo opportunity then?'

'Well, that is not really for me to say,' said Tim, always aware of his position. Having had it ground into him from an early stage in his career, he knew that one must never say anything to undermine the Minister of the day to a member of the public, or worse, a member of the press.

'My reason for raising it was to ask if you would like to be put on the invitation list, Hazel.'

'What, go down to Wales, you mean?'

'Yes. The department will be hosting a dinner afterwards, in conjunction with the Welsh Authorities, you would also be invited to that, of course. But, given the distances involved you will presumably want to find hotel accommodation down there and I'm afraid your magazine will need to pay for that itself.'

'Will you be there?' Hazel found herself asking.

'Certainly. I have the honour to be one of the Department's personnel chosen to organise this event.' Tim smiled at the silliness of the official language. He knew Hazel understood exactly what he meant, but protocol prevented him from putting it any other way. He was already going out on a bit of a limb in inviting Hazel along himself, but he knew responsibility for drawing up the guest list was bound to fall to him when Patrick Blenny shared out the tasks.

-ooOOoo-

As he predicted, the job of organising pretty much all of the trip fell on Tim's shoulders.

His Welsh counterparts were fortunately very well organised, and had set up everything to do with the dinner, and booked rooms for all except the journalists, in the hotel where the event was to be held. Tim looked the hotel up and found it was part of a large group and although not luxurious was, at least, very convenient for travel to the isolated facility they would be visiting. Coaches were also booked, and a taxi company was alerted to be ready to attend to the needs of the journalists.

'I'm not going to be able to stay in the hotel where the dinner is being held, though,' Hazel explained. 'It is over my allocated budget for that sort of thing. But this other place the Welsh people sent details of looks all right, so I think I'll book myself in there for the night of the dinner.'

'Well,' said Tim, now feeling very embarrassed. 'I shall have to be down there for the previous night as well, so two nights away.' Tim let out an embarrassed cough. 'You see my boss will be travelling down with the rest of the party by train and it is my job to meet them there and make sure everything is ready for them, so I'll need to go the night before.'

'I see' said Hazel.

'And I wondered … well, it occurred to me that … perhaps you might like to come down the night before as well, and … erm, we could try out the restaurant in the main hotel together before the crowds descend.'

'Wouldn't you have to eat with the Welsh organisers?'

'Not as I understand it. I should have to dine alone that night.'

Hazel drew in breath ready to make a cutting remark, but Tim hurried on.

'Oh dear. That didn't come out right at all. I didn't mean to infer that I was inviting you along so I didn't have to dine alone. What I meant was that I should very much like you to be my guest for dinner …'

'Your guest? You are inviting me out to dinner?'

'Yes. That is if you would like to … I mean completely understood and so forth if you would rather not … I didn't mean to …'

'I should be delighted,' said Hazel decisively, after a moment's thought. 'And would you mind if we also had a bit of a look round the facility before the gang arrive, just so I can get an idea of what it is all about?'

'You would? Yes … Yes. Certainly, we can do that. No problem!'

Hazel decided that she would confront Tim about his wife during their dinner.

-oooOoo-

THREE

The gas levels were still right down, Ewan reported.

'I don't understand it, Dai,' he said. 'The volumes are the same or slightly up even, but where is all the gas going?'

'Damn it. This would happen now, what with all these big-wigs coming to crawl all over the place. There must be a ruddy leak somewhere. We are going to have to do an inspection.'

-ooOOoo-

The four-star hotel which was hosting the dinner was about a mile and a half further down the hill from the facility, and on the edge of a popular small tourist town.

The other hotel, offered as a cheaper option to the journalists, where Hazel would be staying, was more of a small bed and breakfast holiday hotel and situated almost on the beach. It was immediately adjacent to the steep path leading to the caravan park that Ewan and Dai could see from the control room.

Although this hotel was only, an admittedly steepish, ten minute walk from their destination, the Welsh authorities had thoughtfully laid on a minibus for the journalists to use, and sent details of collection and drop off times with the booking confirmations.

Whilst it did not have the dining facilities or easy access to the town which the other hotel could boast, it did have a large carpark and was just a few steps from the beach and a small amusement arcade, which also sold inflatable beach toys and buckets and spades. Perhaps more importantly, there was also a pub that served food.

Hazel decided to hire a car and drive down to the event, and she asked Tim to join her.

'Well, that is very kind of you,' he said. 'But you must let me pay half the cost and do some of the driving.'

'No, that's all right, Tim. My company will pay for the hire car but, for insurance purposes, I'll have to drive it so, if you don't mind, I'll do the driving.'

'Well, if you are sure,' Tim said. 'Although it seems to be putting you to an awful lot of trouble. If you would rather not have a passenger, I am able to take the train at the Department's expense.'

'Nonsense,' said Hazel. 'It is the least I can do to even things up for the no doubt expensive dinner you are going to buy me!'

And I wonder, thought Hazel, what his wife will have to say when she sees that lot on the credit card statement at the end of the month!

-oo0Ooo-

'This is going to be a great profile raiser,' said Piers Aubin as the Committee members began to leave the meeting. 'I think you should have a professional photographer there, Amanda, and have a press release ready to hand out.'

'I had assumed my civil servants would have organised that sort of thing as a matter of course, Piers, although perhaps we should check.'

'What is it you call them, Amanda? The Mushrooms? I wouldn't trust them to think out all those details. Why don't you leave that to me?'

'Thank you, Piers, and you are quite right,' smiled Amanda. 'I find "The Mushrooms" is the ideal name for them. They hardly inspire confidence as they bumble about in the dark do they, but they always seem to be there spoiling the outlook in some way. And it doesn't seem to matter how often you deal with them, they pop up again in some new area each time you mow them down.'

Patrick Blenny or 'Chief Mushroom' as Amanda Trunnion called him behind his back, approached them now.

'Could we just go over some of the arrangements again, Minister?' he bleated.

'I have to get back to the House,' said Amanda brusquely. 'Can you go through it all with Piers, please. You don't mind, do you Piers? There is an important debate I think the PM expects me to attend and I shouldn't miss it.'

'But,' said Patrick Blenny.

'All right, if you think so,' said Piers Aubin and began to regret making himself quite so available.

-oooOooo-

Nigel and Alison Bannister knew what they had to do to set the caravan up when they arrived on a camp site, but they were not very organised and kept tripping over each other.

'The switch to turn the power on isn't working Nigel.'

'That is because I haven't plugged it in to the site electricity yet. I can't find the big thing with the orange wire wrapped round it.'

'Isn't it in the box at the front with the gas bottles?'

'Hang on I've found it. What on earth was it doing in the shower?'

'Where is the thingy to join the gas bottles to the van Nigel?'

'Well, it is not in the shower, so perhaps it is in the most logical place, the gas locker.'

'No, I've just looked in there.'

'Well, let's think. I took it out when I took the gas bottles to be refilled last Saturday, and I put it … Oh good lord! … I think I might have left it on the bench in the garage.'

'Oh Nigel, you plonker! How are we going to cook supper now?'

'They will probably have another one in the office.'

'But they are shut until the morning.'

'Ah well, we could have a barbecue perhaps.'

'You can't barbecue beef curry and rice, and that is all we have got until I can get to the shops in the morning.'

'I guess we will have to go to the pub for supper then.'

'Nigel, you did remember to pick up my jacket and put it in as I asked, didn't you? It is not in the wardrobe … where did you put it?'

'Well, it's not a cold evening, Alison. I'm sure you will be OK with just a jumper.'

'Nigel! You twerp! You forgot, didn't you?'

'Have you seen the key for the little flap where you plug the fresh water hose in, Alison?'

'It is probably on the bench in the garage with the gas bottle thingy. No, hang on, I've remembered. It is in the pocket of my jacket. The one you forgot to pick up.'

'Ah.'

-ooOoo-

'I've been upgraded Tim!'

'Pardon?'

'The hire car. When I went to pick it up, rather than give me one of those cute little Fiats that I booked, They upgraded me to a Ford Focus,' said Hazel. 'It's in a rather smart blue, too.'

'Very nice,' said Tim who, not being very interested in cars, would have been hard pressed to tell the difference.

'Yes, and on a long journey we will now be much more comfortable.'

The arrangements were coming together nicely, both for Amanda Trunnion's party, travelling in two days' time on the train, and for Tim and Hazel, leaving early tomorrow morning from Hazel's flat, now in a blue Ford Focus.

Tim had been over the plans with his Welsh counterparts again and was confident that he had all the bases covered, and as he packed his suitcase, he felt a little thrill of excitement as he thought of the journey with Hazel and then their cosy dinner tomorrow night.

He hadn't been on anything resembling a date for over twenty years.

-ooOoo-

FOUR

'Nothing?' said Dai.

'Not a trace.' Ewan scratched his head in confusion.

'I don't get this at all. The volumes are slightly up again but the gas level has dropped even more, and yet there seems to be no leak anywhere,' Dai stated.

Methane gas is lighter than air and can 'float' in a cloud in the right conditions. It has no smell or taste, but in the right concentration it is highly explosive.

'I'll have to call Environmental Services, and warn the Met Office. There must be a lot of it by now and we don't want something horrible to happen in a cloud of it.'

'But they can't search the entire pipeline. It's over thirty miles long,' Ewan was concerned now.

'But every single monitoring unit in the whole length of the thing is registering normal levels until you get to here, right at the end, when the levels drop dramatically.'

'I've got the maintenance team installing secondary monitoring in case it's just a faulty meter. They should have one or two new monitoring stations up and running by late afternoon.'

'That will find it,' said Ewan. 'I'll bet it's more dodgy monitoring equipment. Do you remember the contractors had an issue with that when the pipeline was built. Maybe they missed one or two when they replaced them.'

'Yes. I'm sure that's what it is, Ewan,' Dai looked a little more cheerful. 'I'd forgotten about that one. There were so many problems and equipment failures during that last phase of construction, it was just one of many things that held it up, but I bet you are right.'

'Yeah, made me laugh that did. Eighteen months late to hand it over and by the time they did, we'd had a general election and the other lot got in, so they couldn't even claim the credit.'

'What? Claim the credit for a massive overspend on a project that arrived so late that even the protestors had gone home?'

Ewan laughed at that one.

'And now we've got another load of politicians and goodness knows who coming to tramp about all over the place, but this time from England!'

'I think I'll wait until the maintenance boys get back in before I pass this up the line. We are going to look a bit silly if we have raised an issue and it is just a dicky meter.'

-ooOOoo-

They decided to drive around the perimeter of the facility on their way to drop Hazel's cases at her hotel before going the mile and a half or so to the hotel where they would be having dinner and where Tim had a room.

'Crikey,' said Hazel as she climbed back into the car after taking a series of photographs. 'It is enormous. I hadn't realised how big it was, or that there was a solar farm here as well.'

'It is quite something, I must admit,' said Tim.

Whilst they had chatted amiably enough during the drive to Wales, Tim was aware of a certain reserve in Hazel's manner. On the journey he put it down to her concentrating on driving, but it did seem that something was troubling her.

They sat in the car by the fence which surrounded the facility and as Hazel looked at the digital photos she had taken, Tim plucked up the courage to ask if anything was wrong.

'Wrong?' she said. 'What could possibly be wrong?'

'Well, I don't know, Hazel, but you seem a little ... different. Have I done something to offend you?'

Hazel squirmed in her seat. She was going to wait until their dinner this evening to deliver her bombshell, but now she felt cornered, and win or lose, she had to speak. She valued Tim's friendship, and yes, she had to admit to herself that she fancied him, but even if it meant spoiling that she had to tell him that she knew.

'Tim,' she said. 'I've really enjoyed getting to know you over these past few months, and I was very flattered when you invited me on this trip. But I know your secret now, and that changes everything.'

'My ... my secret?'

'Yes, Tim. I had hoped that we ... that you and I ... but I'm not ... I mean it was dishonest of you ...'

'What are you talking about?' said Tim.

'Oh come on, Tim. It is no good trying to play the innocent. I know you are married, and if you are hoping I will be your bit on the side, I've got news for you. Nothing doing!'

'What!' exploded Tim. 'Good grief, Hazel. Is that what you thought? It is nothing like that at all!'

Hazel slumped in her seat. In a rush she realised she had been wrong to think that Tim was interested in her, and now she felt very foolish.

'You didn't think we ... you weren't interested? ... I have made a fool of myself, haven't I. Oh Tim, I'm so sorry ...'

'No Hazel. You are getting this all wrong ... please let me explain.'

'I feel such an idiot ...'

'There is no need, but I do need to explain about my marriage, and then perhaps you will feel differently.'

'Tim, I ...'

'Twenty odd years ago I met and married Claire. We were both just 21 years old and at university, and there was a reason we did it, which was to help her resolve a problem. You see Claire was bought up as a strict Roman Catholic in an Irish family, and I was somewhat loosely Church of England. Claire's parents objected strongly to her marriage to anyone other than a practicing Roman Catholic and, being very young, we did it partly to rebel against them. We hadn't known each other very long but her parents forbade her to see me, so we eloped. I suppose it was to spite them, but needless to say they were very upset and refused to even let Claire into the house. We had to stay with an old aunt of mine as we had nowhere else to live, and we were in dire straights when we both finished University. Claire's parents did at least continue to fund her education but told her that after that they would not support her.'

'But you are still ...'

'Yes, Hazel. Claire and I are still married, but I have not lived with her since we both turned 24. The strictures of her faith forbid divorce, you see, but she also finds it convenient to present herself as a married woman in her career and particularly to her parents and family. Claire will not grant me a divorce, although she has lived with her partner for many years. Her parents are elderly now and she worries that it would kill them if they realised that her partner is a woman. Once they are no longer with us, things might change.'

'Oh dear. I really have made a mess of this, haven't I, Tim. I'm so sorry ...'

'I was going to tell you all this tonight, when we have our dinner, Hazel, and ask you if it would be possible for us to ... to go on a proper date.'

'Oh Tim! Yes, I would like that very much ... very much indeed.'

Somewhat awkwardly, in the confined space of the car, Tim and Hazel embraced and shared their first kiss.

-ooOoo-

Nigel and Alison Bannister ordered fish and chips in the pub by the beach and Nigel offered Alison his jacket in case she was cold.

After some difficulty Nigel had managed to pick the lock of the little flap that covered the fresh water inlet and been able to fill up the water tank.

As they sat in the slightly down-at-heel pub, waiting for their supper, the caravan, now connected to mains electricity, was gradually heating the water which filled the built-in hot water tank, so Alison could have a shower before bed.

'I can't believe you forgot all that stuff, Nigel,' said Alison. 'It is not as though this is the first time we have used the caravan. You should have got the hang of it by now! We should have got a microwave, as I told you, when we bought it. Then we could have heated up the curry I made. But, oh no, you didn't want to spend any more money on it, so now we only have one way to cook ...'

'Tomato ketchup?' said Nigel as their greasy looking supper arrived.

-ooOOoo-

'What time will the car pick me up again, Patrick?'

Amanda Trunnion MP was on the phone to her chief Civil Servant, finalising the arrangements. It had not occurred to her that, at half past eight in the evening, her Officers might be off duty.

Patrick, holding his phone in one hand and stirring his warming mushroom casserole, which his wife had left on the stove for him with the other, went through the arrangements with his boss for a third time.

'If only she would write things down in her diary or something,' he complained to his wife as the call ended. 'I sent her a memo with all this in it, but she left it on her desk of course, and then claims she couldn't find it. She really is the worst one we have had yet, and that includes old Dopey Fish-Face three years ago!'

-ooOOoo-

Tim had put in a quick call to the big hotel where he was due to spend the night, and cancelled the table for two booked for dinner.

He hoped claiming 'travel delays' would sound convincing enough, and left it at that.

He had not expected matters to develop quite as quickly as they had when he helped Hazel carry her cases up to her room in the hotel down by the beach, but he was very, very happy that they did.

Hazel stepped out of the shower swathed in towels.

'Come back to bed,' he said. So she did.

-ooOOoo-

Nigel was paying the bill in the pub when it happened.

All sorts of things went through his mind as the windows outside lit up with a yellow light and two huge bangs, one after the other, shook the building. But instinct for self-preservation kicked in and he threw himself on the floor, and banged his head on the brass foot rail surrounding the bar.

-ooOOoo-

'Tim!' shrieked Hazel.

'Oh Hazel!' murmured Tim into the pillow.

'Half a caravan has just shot past the window!' Hazel informed him, as the room, bathed in an eerie yellow light came back into focus.

-ooOOoo-

'Bloody hell!' said Ewan, letting his fork slip from his nerveless fingers as, dinner forgotten, he grabbed his jacket and ran to his car to get to the control centre.

-ooOOoo-

FIVE

'Well, that explains where all the gas went,' said Dai. 'The Fire-Chief agrees that the leak was down where the pipe crosses the stream over by the old mine. The gas collected there and drifted into the hollow where the caravan park is. Something must have ignited it there.'

'Bloody miracle that nobody was killed,' said Ewan. 'That caravan park is usually quite full at this time of year.'

'Have you looked at the old mine?' asked Dai. 'One of the towers has gone and by the look of it the building at the pit head just blew apart! There is a huge rip in the side of our silo too!'

'And look at the cliff where you can just see down towards the beach by the path ... there are bits of caravans and all sorts of debris all over the place! And look at the pipe ... it is torn right open and a chunk of it is missing!'

-ooOOoo-

When they got back from A&E, Nigel and Alison checked themselves into the hotel by the beach, next door-but-one to the pub where they had been having dinner when the explosion happened.

The amusement arcade which separated the two buildings and sold buckets and spades and beach toys was all but destroyed. It caught fire when half a caravan landed on its flimsy roof.

There was debris everywhere, particularly up the side of the cliff with its little path leading to the remains of the caravan park. Alison shook her head as she surveyed the scenes of destruction from the window of the hotel. Across the car park there was a blue Ford partially submerged under bits of caravan. Their own brown Ford and their caravan were history, blown to smithereens by the gas explosion.

'At least the car was insured,' she said. 'The caravan insurance was separate from that, wasn't it, Nigel?'

'Ah,' said Nigel and closed the bathroom door behind him.

'Nigel?' Alison clenched her fists and pounded on the door, 'Come out here, I want to kill you!'

-oooOoo-

'Well, it was quite a night. It was very lucky that none of the six caravans stored down there was occupied, and only one touring caravan was on the site. They are all write-offs now, of course, although fortunately the couple who were staying there were in the pub by here when the explosion happened. One suffered minor injuries and both they and the hotel staff were treated for shock, but there was no need to admit any of them to hospital and they were bought back to the hotel in the early hours of this morning.'

'Thanks, Bryn. That is a big relief. Ewan here was up at the control centre within minutes of it happening because he only lives over the way, like, so he was able to shut the plant down, but as you can see when the pipe ruptured there was quite a lot of damage and mess.'

'Smelly too,' said Bryn, removing his fireman's helmet and

tucking it under his arm. 'Going to take quite a bit of clearing up, that is.'

'Someone will have to tell those dignitaries who are coming here this afternoon, Dai,' said Ewan.

'Oh crikey, I had forgotten about them … what is the time now … they are due here in about three hours!'

-ooOoo-

Hazel had two urgent jobs to do.

She had to explain to the hire car company why their nice blue Ford Focus now had a tangle of metal and wood, which was once most of a caravan, seemingly inextricably attached to its front end, although the car was not being driven at the time.
Hazel could state, however, that she saw the caravan in question, or rather half of it, flying through the air past her hotel window a second or two before the impact.

She also had to phone the news desk at her office in London and file the story of the unlikely events she had witnessed last night down in Wales.

Tim, they decided, should get a taxi and having extracted his bag from the back of the Ford Focus through the hatchback, which had fortunately popped open when the impact happened, he made for the large hotel where the reception was due to take place. During the short drive he ignored the taxi driver's gabbled questions, and made urgent phone calls to his colleagues to tell them what had happened.

When he arrived, he intended to check in and deposit his bag in the room, so hopefully nobody would realise he did not spend the night there.

Neither Tim nor Hazel explained what they were doing at the precise moment that the explosion took place, of course, although it was not the sort of thing that either of them would ever be likely to forget.

-ooo0oo-

On the train, about an hour and a quarter out of London, when Patrick Blenny told Amanda Trunnion what Tim had just told him via mobile phone, the air turned blue.

The first-class carriage was about a third full of the entourage travelling to Wales to visit the facility. Fortunately, there were no journalists aboard to report the lengthy stream of invective released by the Minister, which would have shocked the teachers at her expensive girls' school.

'Where are the rest of The Mushrooms?' she asked, when she had calmed down a bit, having taken out her frustrations on poor old Patrick. 'I need to find out what we can do about this.'

'If you mean the other Civil Servants, Minister, they are travelling in the second-class carriage next door, shall I fetch them?'

'Yes. Why are they in there?'

'Their employment grade does not entitle them to first-class travel, Minister, so they are on second-class tickets.'

'Right ... well go and gather them up. We need to tell them what has happened.'

-ooo0oo-

SIX

'Now we have to make some decisions,' Amanda Trunnion said to the inner circle sitting around her on the train. 'I didn't want anything to do with this visit to Wales in the first place, it feels like promoting an initiative dreamed up by the last Labour Government. Now, do we call the thing off, get off the train and go back to London? We are going to look bloody silly if we get there to admire the scene of an explosion.'

'I'm all for turning back. This is a waste of time!' said Sir Jacob Mortimer, the Chairman of the Commission.

'Me too,' said Bethany Ford from the National Farmers Union, and Sir Barton Parish, the head of the Highways Agency in England, nodded in agreement.

'There is some very interesting industrial history in that part of Wales, I was rather looking forward to it,' said Professor Potts.

'It is going to be a complete PR disaster if we go down there and get involved with this ruddy explosion,' said Philip Knowles from the Environment Agency.

'Not necessarily,' said Piers Aubin, pushing aside his paper cup of coffee. 'I think we can turn this to our benefit, and for you,

Minister, it could be the coup of a lifetime …'

'What on earth are you babbling about Piers?' Amanda was becoming very red in the face.

'If you will allow me to explain, Minister, this could do you no end of good if carefully managed ….' Aubin was on his feet now and moving to stand in the central aisle as the Civil Servants condemned to endure the privations of second-class travel started to file into the carriage.

All heads turned towards him as he began to set out his idea.

-ooOOoo-

Tim had time to compose himself and ate a little breakfast at the large hotel before meeting two of his Welsh counterparts, who were due to work with him to check everything was ready for the forthcoming event.

'Oh my God, this is terrible,' said Gwen, the first to arrive. 'I took a quick drive past on the way here. What a bloody mess!'

'I was down there earlier,' said Tim. 'It was a hell of an explosion.'

'I wouldn't have liked to be anywhere near that,' said Gwen. 'It must have been terrifying, and it stinks to high heaven as well!'

'Well, I suppose it would. There was a lot of debris, and a fire in one of the shops down on the beach too.'

'Was there? I haven't been down there yet. Do you think our respective Ministers will want to go through with this, or do you think they will cancel?'

'I've no idea,' said Tim. 'The phone lines must be red-hot between their offices right now. I wonder what is going on.'

'Well, here comes Gareth, my boss. He might know.'

'And I see the first of the journalists is arriving,' Tim nodded towards the hotel lobby doors. 'That is Hazel Trigg from The

Gazette in London coming through the doors ... And so it begins.'

-ooOOoo-

Piers Aubin loved nothing better than to have an audience, and now he was in his element.

'If the Minister will agree,' he stated, 'I believe we should continue down to Wales as planned but, of course, with a different agenda when we get there.'

'Have I missed something, Minister?' puffed Patrick Blenny, as the last of the party crammed into the aisle of the first class carriage.

'Probably,' said Amanda. 'Let's hear your idea, Piers.'

'Right, thank you. You see it is quite simple to turn this completely on its head and very much to our advantage. The facility we are going to visit was a flagship project for the previous Labour Government, combining as it did co-working with their Welsh counterparts and creating closer bonds, as they saw it, across a united UK. The project was some years in the development stages and involved close co-operation with the European Union, which provided much of the funding in return for the adoption of the now familiar EU tendering process, which at that time was in its infancy.'

'Where is this all going, Piers? Get to the point,' spluttered Sir Jacob Mortimer.

'I'm just coming to the nub of the matter, Sir Jacob, if you will allow me ...'

Sir Jacob indicated that he should continue.

'The point is that those early EU tendering rules virtually forced the two Governments to accept the lowest tendered price to build it. To secure such a prestigious project the contractors would have fought tooth and nail, cutting who knows what corners, to secure the work at the lowest possible price. Now that we are no longer part of the EU, Minister, we are not bound by those tendering rules and could have procured the work in a different way if the situation was happening now. We could put forward a case to say that the English and Welsh Labour Governments of the day were hoodwinked into commissioning a shoddy, and as it turns out, dangerous, facility by having to comply with EU rules and accepting the lowest tendered price. There is major political capital to be made out of that, Minister, and we will be right on the spot, with a selection of journalists looking at us, to make that point imminently.'

Piers looked around him as if expecting applause or at least supportive comments. Professor Potts was the first to speak.

'The flaw in your argument as I see it, dear boy, is that without the EU providing the funding the project could never have got off the ground in the first place. Naturally they wanted some control of how their money was to be spent so it was obvious that their tender process would need to be followed.'

'Good point, Professor,' said someone from the back of the carriage. 'We couldn't have done it without the EU bankrolling us.'

'But the story we have to tell today is one of shoddy workmanship under a shaky alliance between two Labour administrations, and we know that the project over-ran and cost much more than the original tender price, so we can demonstrate Labour mismanagement!' Piers added as his final flourish.

To some muttering from the back of the carriage, Amanda Trunnion MP, now standing, drew herself up to her full height.

'There is something in this Piers. This opportunity is too good to waste,' she said quietly, so that only those closest to her could hear, before she took a deep breath. 'Right, ladies and gentlemen, we continue on to Wales as planned,' she announced at the top of her voice.

-oo0Ooo-

Hazel looked around the hotel lobby and selected a seat where she could order a coffee and watch proceedings from a good vantage point.

She had seen Tim talking to a dumpy little woman on the other side of the lobby but, as they had agreed it might be for the best, she did not acknowledge him as their eyes met.

The plan was probably going to change in the light of events, but the idea was that the journalists would meet at the hotel and then travel by minibus to the site. After a tour round, and a bit of pontificating from the politicians, they would come back in the minibus again for a 'presentation' with questions and answers and then collect information packs about the project before supper was served in a big dining room reserved for the event.

Hazel asked her taxi driver to detour around the site itself so that she could take some 'after' pictures to go with the 'before' collection she had taken when she and Tim arrived. She now felt well prepared to submit very different copy from that which was originally envisaged, and she allowed herself a little smile as she realised she had quite a story to tell.

-oo0Ooo-

SEVEN

Patrick explained the new plan to Tim by phone as their train journey continued.

The focus now, as so often in the recent past, was to paint the EU as the bad guy in the process and shift the blame for the explosion onto their tendering process.

A quick internet search revealed that the contract to build the facility was secured by a consortium of contractors headed by the French company, Bolas, supported by the Welsh company A B Jones and Sons (Swansea), to satisfy the 'local labour' requirement, and the now disbanded English 'Team 5' Civil Engineering Group.

The contract was let after a lengthy tender process and involved some re-negotiation to get the specification and phasing requirements down to a level that the Welsh and English Governments of the day could accept.

The construction operation was funded largely by phased investments from the EU, based on something called 'Key Performance Indicators' designed to keep the building operations on track. Despite that, the project was handed over eighteen months late and very considerably over budget, and the legal claims the various companies lodged against each other, to shift the blame, took some years to be resolved.

Having said all that, the concept of the project really was ground breaking.

It would combine power generation and state of the art sewage processing to put energy back into the grid in the form of electricity via a biogas powered turbine, and produce a run off into the sea, which was said to be so clean you could drink it. Nobody believed that of course, but for a while the plant did function and perform well.

As a result the current Government were looking into re-branding it as something of their own. They were considering the potential for announcements about case studies to look into rolling versions of it out in various locations around the UK, as part of a massive new 'green' initiative.

Before the explosion disrupted those plans, Amanda Trunnion MP was being sent down to the facility to begin the process of raising public awareness that such initiatives could work and were being considered by the present Government. She may not have been the most reliable pair of hands for such an initiative, but it was a start.

-ooOoo-

'And with the main contractor being French,' Piers Aubin was saying, 'we can direct any fire away from the English companies involved. Everyone is suspicious of the French, so emphasising that they led the project will stoke up the masses even more, especially when we tell them it was eighteen months late and way over budget.'

'So, we can take a swipe at the EU for its over-complex tendering process and make the point that, after Brexit, we no longer have to follow their rules.' Amanda Trunnion was warming to this idea more and more.

'That is going to really impress the cabinet when they see what you have done with this, Amanda!'

'Yes, Piers, I think it might. Now, where is the Chief Mushroom, I'm going to need a new press release and a re-write of my speech.'

-ooOoo-

'They are going to say what!' said Gareth incredulously. 'Oh, good grief.'

'The First Minister will have something to say about this … I've left a message for the local Member of the Senedd to call me back. He'll be on his way here now for the tour,' said Gwen.

'How do you think they will take it?' asked Tim.

'Not well, I'd say,' Gareth was shaking his head. 'You see the Welsh haven't had much to smile about lately, what with one thing and another, and we were all pretty proud of this project. Gave us a bit of national pride, it did. It helped with the politicians' credibility to be able to point to it as an achievement.'

'And now this has happened,' added Gwen. 'There will be all sorts of awkward questions, which probably won't do Anglo-Welsh relations any good at all.'

Tim exchanged concerned looks with his Welsh counterparts but then, as he now had to re-write and print off an element of the hand-out pack that would be given to the journalists, he took himself off to his room to get it done.

-ooOoo-

EIGHT

Hazel was waiting in the lobby by the lifts when Tim returned.

'Oh, hello Hazel,' he said. 'Were you looking for me?'

'Yes, Tim. Look you have got to tell the journalists what is going on. There are ten or a dozen in the hall now, including national newspaper people, and more on the way. They have all heard about what happened, of course, so they are coming here in droves.'

'Have the Welsh people said anything to them?'

'Other than that "a statement will be issued shortly," no. They have scuttled off somewhere to talk to their Minister who has just arrived.'

Tim looked at his watch.

'The train will be arriving in the next few minutes. I was supposed to be on the coach to meet them, but my boss told me to stay here and get the press pack re-written. The receptionist should be printing them off for me now.'

'Well, best you get over to Reception. If these press boys get a sniff that the details are being printed there, they will tear the place apart to get the first copies.'

'Oh dear. Yes, I see what you mean. Would you excuse me, Hazel,' Tim was heading for the door. 'And thank you … thank you very much.'

-ooo0oo-

'Minister, I think there are some press people on the station,' said Patrick as the train slowed to a halt. 'They must have worked out you would be on this train.'

'Oh bugger,' said Amanda. 'That means I'll have to say something without the Welsh people alongside. Does my hair look all right?'

'You could just say that a statement will be released shortly and that you are on your way to see the Welsh Minister,' said Patrick.

'Yes … yes. Very good Patrick. That ought to hold them. Make sure The Mushrooms all know that is our line, and to keep their mouths shut.'

Amanda took a deep breath.

'Everybody … Everybody … Listen please. The press are on the platform and I will deal with them. Please do not talk to them or make any comment. We will be issuing a statement shortly and I am on my way to see the Welsh Minister, so please say nothing before then without reference to me.'

-ooo0oo-

Nigel and Alison Bannister were waiting on the platform when Amanda Trunnion MP's train was due in. They were going in the opposite direction, back home.

'Look at all those photographers on the other side of the platform,' observed Alison. 'Do you suppose somebody famous is coming on the train?'

'I think I know what they are,' said Nigel. 'They are press people, probably here to write about the explosion. That gives me an idea …'

'Nigel? Nigel, where are you going? Come back! The train will be here any minute!'

-ooOOoo-

Hazel had asked her office to text her if anything new broke about the story of the explosion, or the Ministerial visit.

Her phone buzzed in her pocket, and as she got it out she read that one of the red-top newspapers had got an exclusive interview with somebody who claimed to be on the site of the explosion, and whose caravan got blown up.

'Oh well,' she thought. 'The Gazette is much more interested in the political angle, so that doesn't matter.'

She had, however, had a quick interview with two of the staff at the hotel over breakfast to capture their experience of the event, so pressing a few keys, she sent the draft of that interview off to her office.

'That ought to disappoint the red-top boys when they realise their on-the-spot exclusive is not so exclusive after all,' she thought.

NINE

Having fended off the reporters on the platform and fought her way through to their coach, Amanda sat down with Piers Aubin in the next seat, and together they started to work out their strategy.

In the seat behind them, Patrick Blenny was on the phone to his office where his staff were in a state of some nervous excitement. It was not often that anything much happened in the Department for Water Supply and Sanitation, let alone anything that meant they made the headlines, and the atmosphere in the office was very tense.

Everyone on the coach seemed to be on their mobile phones. Some reassuring relatives and spouses, some to their offices, and one or two of the more militant junior civil servants were whispering into their phones to contacts outside the office, or employees in the offices of other political parties, and looking furtively about them as they did it.

-ooo0oo-

Tim had managed to prevent any of the newly printed copies of the 'press pack' from escaping, or falling into the wrong hands, and having removed the obsolete pages, he was now in the dining room, sorting them into the individual folders ready to be issued when the time came.

He became aware that Hazel was peeping around the corner of a door.

'Mr. Blande, isn't it? Could I have a word?'

'It's all right, Hazel, nobody else is here. Come in.'

'Right, sorry. Look I've got to leave with the journalists for the site tour in a minute, but I just quickly wanted to tell you that the car hire company have been very good about it and will be delivering a replacement car here this afternoon, so you are all right for a ride back home tomorrow.'

'Well, that is good news, Hazel, but in the light of events, the Minister and my boss might expect me to travel back on the train with them. We will have to see how it unfolds.'

'Oh. Yes, I see how that might happen. Fair enough. You will be all right here in this hotel tonight, though Tim. It is much nicer than the one down by the beach.'

'I would rather be down there with you, Hazel.' Tim blushed to his roots.

'I'd like that too, Tim. Maybe when we get back to London, we can fix-up that proper date you talked about.'

'Yes, please …' said Tim as the door opened and one of the Welsh officers announced that the entourage of journalists was just about to leave to meet the politicians on the site.

'I dunno if you have got a mask or a scarf or something, but it don't half stink down there!' he added.

-ooo0oo-

Only Professor Potts was not on his mobile phone on the coach. Having lost his wife five years previously, there was nobody at home to be worried whether he had survived the explosion or not when the initial details appeared on the morning news.

Instead, he was interested in looking at the scenery from the coach window as they traveled the short distance to the damaged facility.

Before leaving London, he had studied the plans of the complex and as more details of the explosion emerged, he wondered if the little mountain stream which tumbled down the cliff to the sea had been affected. As they approached the perimeter of the site, he took out the small pair of binoculars he always carried in case there was any interesting bird life to see, and tried to focus in on the area where he knew the vast pipe crossed the stream.

Even at this distance, what met his eye was horrendous.

The once sparkling clear bubbling stream was now a brown sludgy smear and he could just make out workmen fighting to stem the pulsing flow of raw sewage gushing from the breached pipe above it.

He knew that the stream met the sea just in front of the small beach adjacent to the hotel where the journalists were due to stay, and putting his binoculars on his lap, he interrupted Patrick Blenny, who was sitting next to him, between phone calls.

What he had to say galvanised the civil servant into action and what followed was a further flurry of phone calls during which Patrick clutched his brow and looked increasingly harassed.

-ooo0oo-

Tim put his phone back in his pocket.

'I'm afraid,' he announced from the front of the first of the minibuses now travelling to the site. 'That there may be a problem with the hotel where those of you who are staying the night had been expecting to stay. However, I am pleased to say that you will be offered accommodation at the hotel where we will be having dinner tonight at no additional cost, although, depending on numbers, we might have to ask one or two of you to share.'

As he made this last point, he caught Hazel's eye and struggled to keep a grin, which matched her own, from his face.

Due to the rapid increase in numbers, there were now three minibuses travelling in convey to the site, and similar announcements were being made by Tim's Welsh counterparts in the other two vehicles, which their civil servants had managed to conjure up at the last minute, to deal with the influx of journalists.

The three minibuses processed around the perimeter of the site and across a part of it on a predetermined route, but because of the debris and the unpleasant smell, the journalists had to be content to take their pictures through the windows until the three vehicles pulled up outside the control centre next to the coach delivering the dignitaries.

-ooOOoo-

Philip Knowles of the Environment Agency, overhearing what Professor Potts and Patrick Blenny were discussing, asked to borrow the Professor's binoculars.

When the Professor told him where to look and he saw the extent of the damage to the stream, he realised that they had a major environmental disaster on their hands, and in two swift phone calls he mobilised a task force through his office, and that of his Welsh counterpart, to assess the situation and begin the clean-up operation.

Above all, he told his second-in-command, the raw sewage spill must not be allowed to continue to flow into the sea.

The coach drove round the perimeter of the site and across a portion of it beside the solar panels to give those on board a good idea of how the site looked. As the coach came to a stop beside the control centre on the old concrete road, Sir Jacob Mortimer, as Chairman of the Commission, led Amanda Trunnion MP down the steps, and holding handkerchiefs to their noses, they headed the dash towards the building where the journalists were assembling.

Once inside with the door firmly shut, and introduced to Dai and Ewan, they asked for a brief synopsis of the damage before they opened the proceedings with the waiting journalists.

'At first we didn't realise about the damage to the waste digester,' explained Dai. 'We thought it was just a methane explosion, but the second biogas explosion happened a split second later.'

'When the pipe blew apart, part of it flew off and cut through the side of the silo,' added Ewan. 'That caused the second gas and raw sewerage escape, and that gas caused the more significant explosion. The sewage explains the lingering smell.'

'The bacteria in the digester, once released to air, multiplied rapidly, you see,' said Dai. 'That is partly what the brown stuff is you can see on the solar panels, the buildings, and the concrete area outside.'

'The rest of that stuff is what it is feeding on. Tons of human sh... I mean sewage, which is why it is breeding so fast,' Ewan explained.

'But,' said Professor Potts, 'it will die off naturally quite shortly when its food source is removed. It cannot live without constantly reproducing and will soon exhaust the available food supply.'

'My God!' said Bethany Ford, from the National Farmers Union, 'What could that horrible bacteria do if it gets onto farmland? Will it eat the crops?'

'No, my dear,' said the Professor reassuringly. 'The agent

is designed to destroy itself after one round of ingestion, reproduction and blooming ... apart from the gas it releases in the process, it is quite harmless.'

'Was this something created in a lab?' asked Amanda Trunnion. 'Is it not natural?'

'Well, it was engineered rather than created as such, Minister,' replied the Professor. 'Think of it as a bit like yeast in that it blooms and dies off at the end of its lifecycle. A bio-digester system like this utilises organic waste, particularly animal and human excreta, to produce fertiliser and biogas. The bio-digester we have here consists of large airtight, high-density silos within which excreta diluted in water flows continuously and is fermented by microorganisms present in the waste. This early example is particularly large, of course, but much smaller versions can now be built which do not require so much infrastructure or so much enzyme to drive the process.'

'But I thought you said it reproduces,' said Bethany Ford.

'Excuse me, Minister,' said Patrick Blenny. 'The press people are becoming rather restless and are complaining about the smell.'

-oo0Ooo-

TEN

'And so,' concluded Amanda, 'the EU's inefficient processes and the creation of the scenario where major projects like this have to be built for the lowest possible tender price, with the inevitable corner cutting that involves, are responsible for the environmental disaster you see before you today. The Welsh and British taxpayer has been hoodwinked into accepting worse than second best in return for what? Debt, bureaucracy and the loss of our Sovereignty. I am only glad that never again will these islands be subject to such overbearing interference. Today, my friends, demonstrates the value of the new era the United Kingdom is embarking upon, free from such strictures! Free to be a United Kingdom and masters of our own destiny once again!'

There was applause, but it has to be said it was rather more muted than Amanda, and her assistant in writing the speech, Piers Aubin, had hoped. But on the whole the clapping drowned out the dissenting voices as, with a flourish, Amanda turned on her heel and marched back to the coach, surprising the dozing driver somewhat who took a second or two to open the doors.

-ooOOoo-

'Er … right,' announced Tim, after a moment of confusion and then consultation, as the English part of the delegation filed out after the Minister and started boarding the coach. 'We will now return to the hotel where the Welsh Minister will address us and information packs will be handed out.'

'Thank you, Tim,' said Gareth. 'I have to tell you our Minister is coming to the boil and is proper annoyed that he was not allowed to speak. I wouldn't be surprised if there isn't an almighty row on the coach. He is a bit fiery, you see, our Kenneth is. Keen EU supporter too, so that last little speech will have rubbed him right up the wrong way. Hopefully he might have simmered down a bit by the time we get back to the hotel.'

-ooOOoo-

'Well, you might at least have allowed me to speak. That was the original plan, after all!'

The diminutive figure of Kenneth Jones MS hardly towered over Amanda Trunnion as she sat in her seat on the coach, and he stood in the aisle, but he had a high and penetrating voice which commanded attention, and he was clearly very annoyed.

'And what was all that guff about "overbearing interference" and the United Kingdom being free of the EU? We never approved all that! You must understand, Minister, that not everyone shares the current loathing of our EU neighbours those from Westminster push so hard down all our throats. I urge you to tone down your language and respect the fact that the English are just one partner in this project, and the cause of the explosion is not even known yet!'

'I assume,' said Amanda, 'that you agree that a root and branch investigation into the causes of this disaster must be launched at once? If you feel that would be something you would like to announce, please feel free to do so when we get back to the hotel where you will have the floor.'

'I will do that, yes. But I must warn you that I am considering lodging a complaint to your Cabinet about this and I must insist that there is no more of this triumphalist rhetoric!'

'Suit yourself,' muttered Amanda under her breath as the Welsh Minister stomped off to resume his seat.

-ooo0oo-

As the minibuses disgorged the journalists and the three civil servants back at the hotel, where mercifully the air was considerably purer and easier to breathe, Hazel took Tim to one side.

'I'd like to volunteer to be one of those having to share a hotel room,' she whispered, with a smirk.

'I'm not sure I'm the one who will get to organise that,' said Tim with a grin. 'But your kind offer is noted.'

'I've had an email from the car-hire company to say they will deliver the new car before five this afternoon, so in the break before dinner I'll nip down to the other hotel and get my stuff, ready to spend the night here.'

'Right-ho,' said Tim. 'I'll go and see what is happening about the hotel rooms when I've handed out the press information packs.'

-ooo0oo-

'And I fundamentally object to the triumphalist rhetoric the English Minister inflicted on us at the facility,' Kenneth Jones MS almost shouted. 'Whilst it may be politically expedient and popular in Westminster, it is simply not fair to dump the blame for this disaster at the door of the European Union. As we speak, we have no idea whatsoever what caused this explosion, and until an independent, root and branch, detailed public enquiry is launched and concluded, anything else is rank political manoeuvring and conjecture. I ask the Minister to withdraw her statement, and to join me in a calm and considered appraisal of what happened, when all the evidence is to hand, so that reasoned and pragmatic conclusions can be drawn, based on the facts, rather than yet more Westminster bluff! Will you now withdraw your statement, Minister?'

And with that he sat down.

Amanda raised herself a little from her chair, but did not stand up.

'Er, no,' she said and sat down again.

-ooOOoo-

'That's torn it,' muttered Patrick. 'Now she is in danger of turning a spat into a major diplomatic incident.'

'Do you think we can stop this?' whispered Tim, at his side.

'We can try, and I'll go down and call the Cabinet Minister and a couple of friendly senior MPs while you hold the fort here, if you don't mind, Tim. But frankly I think she has gone too far, and there will be a lot of mopping up to do.'

Tim sighed, and getting to his feet as Patrick quietly left the room, he prepared himself to take charge.

'Thank you, ladies and gentlemen. There will now be a short question and answer session and then an opportunity for photographs in the reception hall, before drinks and dinner will be served next door. As is usual on these occasions, please could you keep your questions short and avoid adding supplemental points so that the Ministers can give clear and concise answers, and so that everyone who wants to gets a chance to ask a question. Please could you state your name and the organisation you represent, and wait until the roving microphone is handed to you before speaking. Thank you.'

'Kieron Howard, Daily Mail,' said the first on his feet.

'This is looking like a major political spat from where I'm standing,' he said. 'We all know the EU are renowned for messing up contracts and burying the details in a blizzard of unnecessary paperwork, but the Welsh Minister, with respect, seems to be taking their side! How can you stand there, Mr. Jones, and say that our membership of the EU was anything other than a complete disaster, when the British people were forced to hand over control of our country to Brussels? Isn't this awful project the absolute demonstration of how much better off we are leaving all that behind us and rebuilding our national pride, as one nation, without the EU looking over our shoulder?'

Next up was Dewi Davies of the Aberystwyth Argus.

'This project by here is the absolute state of the art in sewage management and without funding from the EU it would never have happened. Granted, the procurement method might have been better, but without access to their funding now, after Brexit, does the English Minister really believe that the UK has any chance of staying in the forefront of innovations such as these, and would it not be better just to admit that without EU membership the British Isles simply cannot compete?'

And so it went on, with increasingly heated exchanges on both sides, until Professor Potts got to his feet and asked if he could make a comment.

The room fell silent when he said 'I don't mean to make any sort of political comment, that is not the role of the scientific community, but can I just ask if our time would not be more usefully spent in discussing how we can clear up the environmental disaster we have just witnessed in a spirit of mutual co-operation, rather than looking for scape-goats on which to pin the blame. Surely the time for recriminations can come later when we have found a way to stop raw sewage pouring into the river and the sea beyond?'

That stopped the debate dead.

'Ah,' said Tim, relieved on having received a signal from the hotel management, 'Although it is a little early, ladies and gentlemen, I can announce that the cocktail bar is open, and if you would like to make your way through the two sets of double doors on your right, the hotel staff will be happy to serve you.'

The predictable rush to the bar left Tim standing in an emptying room as Patrick Blenny approached him.

'Well done, Tim. What a rabble!'

With a nod Tim agreed.

'Bit of news on the sleeping arrangements,' Patrick announced.

'It has been decided that I will double up with you tonight, as I understand there are two beds in your room. Hope you don't mind, but they have arranged it so that at least the Senior staff can stay together. I'm sure neither of us would like to be sharing with juniors, or worse still any of these horrendous journalists,' he laughed.

What Tim thought about that, he kept to himself.

-ooOoo-

ELEVEN

As the little Fiat jiggled its way down the quiet Welsh roads, Tim told Hazel a little more about what had happened to him the night before.

'And honestly, even in scout camp as a boy, I have never known anyone fart as much as Patrick Blenny! He even farted when he was asleep, and made no bones about letting one rip while cleaning his teeth with the bathroom door ajar this morning. It was like being imprisoned with a demented whoopee cushion!'

'Oh bad luck, Tim!' Hazel laughed. 'I guess I was very lucky, at least in comparison to that. I got paired up with Susan Snarky, I mean Starkey, of the Birmingham Post. All she did of any note was talk for about an hour and a half to her friend on her phone, running down all their mutual friends and criticising everything from their handbags and dress sense to their choice of current boyfriend. I think political reporting was all a bit new to her, and she had come down with another bloke from the paper. I got the distinct impression that sharing a room with him, rather than me, had been the original plan.'

'I was not the only one who would have preferred a different sharing partner, then.'

'Never mind. When we get back to London and have that proper date we have been talking about, maybe another chance to share will come up.'

'Not separate rooms then?'

'I only have a studio flat, Tim. The only separate room is the bathroom. Although if you behave like Mr. P. Blenny, you will be spending the night in there. That is, if you are by any chance, invited to stay-over.'

'I promise nothing like that will happen, although avoiding a curry for our proper date might be wise.'

'Well, I'm not saying you are invited, yet. We will have to see how good you are at spoiling a girl on a date first. And by the way, I don't like curry, I was hoping for something a bit closer to 'fine dining' than that.'

This good-natured banter followed a period during which Tim had made haste as slowly as he could to clear up the paperwork and the last debris of the events of the previous evening, so that almost all the guests, the journalists, and most certainly all of Amanda Trunnion's party had left, before he too was ready to leave.

Patrick Blenny had been happy to leave Tim in charge of finalising matters, signing off the bill and so on, and made a play of needing to return the Minister to Westminster for a meeting with the Chief Whip as soon as practically possible.

For her part Amanda was also eager to get away and was looking forward to her interview with the Whip. She expected she was about to be congratulated, following the events of the last couple of days.

-ooOOoo-

As planned, during the drinks break before the evening meal, Hazel had collected her baggage in the replacement hire car.

It had turned out to be one of the small retro-style Fiat models she had originally tried to hire. She had dealt with the car company's paperwork and returned to the larger hotel in good time for the start of the meal, while her colleagues were still drinking their cocktails.

Now, after breakfast and away from prying eyes, Tim and Hazel had made their escape together in the little car.

'Not quite as comfortable as that Ford Focus, is it.' Hazel stated as they joined the motorway.

'Oh, I don't know,' said Tim, taking a more critical look around the interior of the car for the first time. 'It seems very stylish, and it nips along quite nicely.'

'I suppose it does, but whilst only having 'ginger-beer money', I am cursed with having Rolls-Royce tastes, you see … You might like to remember that, when planning our proper date,' chuckled Hazel.

As she drove along, Hazel made a mental note to arrange to visit the doctor. The issue of contraception must be addressed if she was going into a relationship again after all these years.

-oo0Ooo-

Amanda Trunnion smiled winningly at the Chief Whip as he ushered her into his office and closed the door. But he did not smile back.

'What,' he questioned, 'the blue-blazes do you think you are playing at?'

Amanda looked at him open mouthed.

'But I thought …'

'Ministers in the Cabinet are up in arms about this, and the PM himself has expressed his displeasure at the reports we have received.'

-ooOOoo-

Professor Potts had not enjoyed the train journey back to London and was glad to be back at his comfortable, but untidy, house on the edge of the countryside.

The bird feeders all needed topping up, he noticed, and there was quite a bit of deadheading to do in the rose borders. He had meant to do that before he had been called away.

First, though, he needed to send emails to arrange to collect together a group of former students and academics who he knew could help him to create practical solutions for decontaminating the site of the damaged facility in Wales. He proposed to present these solutions to the English and Welsh Governments and seek to engage them in a programme to clean up the mess.

He turned on his computer and went to make a cup of tea while it warmed up.

TWELVE

Tim was quite pleased with the arrangements he had made.

The tickets for Les Misérables were booked and so was a corner table, not too near the band, in Brasserie Zédel on Sherwood Street, not far from the theatre.

Tim had read about Brasserie Zédel, but never been there himself. Apparently it was "a grand Parisian Brasserie with an authentic Art Deco interior", in a basement, in the heart of Piccadilly. Appropriately, in keeping with its decorative style, it had a band playing subtle "foot tapping 1920s jazz music", and served "traditional French food at reasonable prices", at least according to the reviews he had found.

Tim knew about London West End restaurants and hoped their idea of 'reasonable prices' was the same as his.

He had agreed that he would pick Hazel up in a taxi at her flat at the specified time, and he had ordered a rather expensive bottle of champagne and some flowers to be delivered earlier in the day.

This being a Saturday, and therefore not when he usually travelled, Tim had to carefully check the train timetables to ensure he arrived in London in good time to travel to Hazel's flat. Not wishing to push his luck, or make any assumptions, he bought an 'open' return train ticket just in case it was difficult to purchase a ticket late at night, if he happened to be returning home after the date.

Now he had to organise what he was going to wear, and he had to decide what to do about the ticklish issue of contraception. In the height of passion they had taken a risk in Wales, but it was undoubtedly irresponsible, and Tim worried about finding a way for the future.

In the hope that matters would develop, he had bought some condoms from the machine in the local pub, but he wondered if Hazel was on the pill or had some other form of contraception.

How on earth do you raise these issues with a woman? Asking for a date is quite stressful enough, but in this modern era all these other difficult questions have to be faced before one can proceed with confidence. 'What a passion killer', thought Tim.

Having not had a date let alone anything else for the best part of twenty years, left Tim uncertain how to broach these subjects and what was expected of him.

He struggled with this issue endlessly. He worried that not asking might offend Hazel, but that asking might offend her too. He was losing sleep worrying about it.

-oo0Ooo-

As he opened the post, Nigel Bannister triumphantly held up a cheque.

'There you are, Alison. I told you it was worth talking to those journalists on the railway station about the explosion, and now we are five hundred pounds better off!'

'Yes,' said Alison. 'But the caravan that you forgot to insure cost the thick end of ten thousand pounds, so that is the thin end of the wedge. I sometimes wonder why I put up with you Nigel. You are hopeless.'

'Ah,' said Nigel. 'I suppose that's fair comment in the light of events. Would you like another cup of tea?'

-ooOoo-

Amanda Trunnion MP sat at her untidy little desk in Portcullis House.

This purpose-built extension to the Houses of Parliament, where many MP's had their offices, was convenient and much more modern than the crumbling offices reserved for their use within the main building itself, and Amanda was lucky to have the use of the space.

She shared the small room, or cell, as she called it, with Frances Banner-Dyer, a backbencher on the right wing of the party with a troublesome constituency in North Yorkshire and a tiny majority gained at the last election. As a result of the precarious nature of her seat, Frances spent most of her time in her constituency trying to shore up relations with the locals. The arrangement suited Amanda well and she usually had the little office to herself.

Today, however, as she slumped into her chair and slipped her shoes off, she was in need of a friend, and would have been grateful for one of Frances's infrequent visits.

Her meeting with the Chief Whip, whilst mercifully short, had been bruising. Worse, as a result, she had had to agree to apologise privately to Kenneth Jones, the diminutive Welsh Minister, and to offer the hand of friendship as part of an enquiry into what had happened at the facility in Wales. He, not she, would lead the enquiry which was bound to attract media attention and put her on the spot.

The Chief Whip knew that, of course, and seemed to take ghoulish pleasure in watching her squirm as she realised what lay ahead.

He had made it abundantly clear that she was to promote and praise the concept, if not the delivery method, of the facility in Wales and hint that a new improved generation of something very like it might be rolled out in the near future under the present Government. But he explained that such facilities were understandably unpopular with the communities in which they were to be built.

'The more of these things we can shove off into Wales, the better the chances of getting planning consent without an almighty row, and without upsetting our own voters,' he explained. 'If the Welsh kick off, it is a Welsh problem, but if the new facilities get supported then it is all our idea ... get it?'

'Yes, I understand,' Amanda had replied meekly.

'Even though it is likely that none of the bloody things will ever actually get built, we can claim it as our initiative and snatch a bit of the 'green agenda' away from the other lot. The strategy here, Amanda, let me be clear on this, is to appear to be creating and driving a major green infrastructure programme, irrespective of whether it actually delivers anything ... get it?'

Once again Amanda confirmed that she got it, and the interview concluded.

She saw that her job was now to promote a 'green' initiative that was highly unlikely ever to deliver anything. It was just a ruse to gain a toe hold on the 'green' agenda, for purely political currency. She was being told to join the world of Westminster 'smoke and mirrors', and she knew that those who had not been able to cope with such manoeuvres were quickly cast into the political wilderness.

Frances Banner-Dyer kept a packet of cigarettes and a lighter in her top drawer.

Although she did not smoke, Amanda slipped on her shoes and

reached in and helped herself. She planned to find a quiet corner of the courtyard where smoking was allowed to calm her frayed nerves.

-ooOoo-

THIRTEEN

Tim could not believe that it had all gone so wrong.

Hazel, when she called him, could hardly speak and was clearly distressed.

The bouquet of flowers he had sent had apparently included several large white lilies which, whilst very attractive, had set off her hay fever to such a degree that she had to cancel their date.

While Hazel streamed and swallowed antihistamines, Tim had called the theatre and tried to sell back the tickets for the show, and cancelled the restaurant reservation.

As he fought to get his money back for the train tickets, Hazel, still sneezing, was putting the lilies in the bin on the street outside her flat.

-oooOoo-

'I'd like you to go and meet the new Home Sec., Lakshmi Prakash, and tell her how you are going to play the situation we talked about yesterday, please. She is very interested and will be monitoring progress,' read the Chief Whip's text.

If Amanda was having her progress monitored by the new Home Sec., she thought, either she was in serious trouble, or this was her chance to make a name for herself. If it was the former of these options, then she was glad that she would not be reporting to the previous Home Sec., who was a vicious little woman who only recently succumbed to pressure to resign after all sorts of problems with the staff in her department.

Mind you, now she came to think about it, she probably wore the same size in jackboots as the new incumbent, so there was not much to choose between them.

Either way, she needed to make the best of this, so she pulled her mobile phone from her pocket and called Piers Aubin.

-oo0Ooo-

Professor Edwin Potts had just finished the dead heading and was about to move on to an inspection of his bee hives at the bottom of his large garden.

He hated mobile phones, but the persistent, exasperating little thing in his pocket buzzed and played its nasty artificial electronic interpretation of Beethoven's Fifth until he pulled it out of his pocket and answered it.

'Potty, my dear old thing!' chirruped Sebastian Burleigh-Marks, as he accepted the call. 'Got your email and so on, and so forth. All jolly instructive and certainly a project one should support. Count me in, old chap. Count me in!'

'Thank you, Sebastian, I hoped you would feel able to join our little band. The task before us is not going to be easy, but I believe we already have the ear and the support of some influential politicians, and if you can handle relationships with them and their colleagues so that we can get on with the work, it should not take us too long to wrap this up.'

'Certainly! Certainly. A great pleasure, and an honour to work with you again, Potty, old man, I must say. Thank you for thinking of me.'

'You were at the top of my list, of course, Sebastian. I shall enjoy our little conversations and be happy to watch the masterful way you deal with your political cronies, if I may use that expression, with such aplomb.'

'Why, you old sweetheart! You are too kind. And there really is nothing to it you know. One little dive into the archives of our time together at Eton or Oxford with most of these politicians usually unearths some gem which, whilst perhaps better left buried and away from the glare of publicity, can be usefully employed to ensure a meeting of minds, shall we say.'

'I hope you are not advocating the use of blackmail, Sebastian,' smiled the Professor.

'Certainly not, Potty, old boy. Heaven forbid. Although it must be said that when trying to press a case, being cursed with a reputation for being scandalously and frequently dragged through the gutter as I am, it can be helpful to remind one's former classmates and college chums that perhaps all the fun we had together in our golden youth is better left under wraps. It certainly helps them to see eye to eye with one's current aims and objectives, as it were!'

'Yes, well. I will leave all that to you, Sebastian, and clearly, as in the past, it will be no concern of mine how you proceed. Similarly, as previously, I take it that we can agree that our … erm … arrangements are confidential and are to remain entirely between us.'

'My dear old chap! That can be taken as read. I don't think anyone has ever discovered that I even attended lectures at your knee, albeit infrequently, so protecting, and if you like concealing, our enduring friendship is a matter of course. Usual terms, I take it?'

'Yes. As you say, our usual terms of business will apply. As before, I will ensure that your club subscription is paid and cover your expenses there during the course of this project. I take it that you are still a member of Osbert's Club in Mayfair?'

'They haven't thrown me out yet, or rather not recently, so yes I can still lay my hat there, Professor.'

'And the politicians still use it to meet and discuss some of the rather more … ah … delicate matters of the day?'

'Certainly, and it is busier than ever. The old brigade are proposing and seconding the new generation of Conservative blots even as we speak, and the lunch and dinner tables heave against the bloated bellies of the great and the supposedly good as fulsomely as ever.'

-ooOOoo-

Philip Knowles rarely took calls on a Saturday, but this was different.

'What do you mean you can't stop it? Can't you just shut off the pipe?' he said.

The joint Welsh and English task force dispatched to deal with the environmental disaster down at the facility in Wales were having problems controlling the flow of raw sewage into the site.

'If we just stop up the pipe, where is it all going to go?' the chief engineer at the plant asked. 'The spare volume in the pipe only has a limited capacity to hold it all, until it either starts to back up or blows the pipe apart. Unless you can think of a way of getting thousands of people not to flush it away for a while it is going to keep on coming.'

'There must be somewhere set aside to divert it to in an emergency.'

'You would think so, wouldn't you. There is only one catch pit and that is already half full. There were going to be several, before the powers that be slashed a chunk out of the budget, so instead of using the land designated for an overflow trap and flash pits, they ended up building a solar park on it.'

'What do you suggest?'

'This is horrible, but I'm not sure we have a lot of choice now. There is an old abandoned deep mine next to the site. We could open it up and lay in temporary pipes at ground level and let it run into there until the plant is repaired …'

'That's a bit extreme. What do the Welsh say about it?'

'The problem as they see it is that the mine is in private ownership. Although it has been abandoned for many years, it still belongs to someone, and we would have to get their permission.'

'Who owns it?'

'The Welsh people are trying to find out.'

FOURTEEN

On Monday, as lunchtime approached, Tim was still in a meeting which seemed to be going on for ever.

The issue under discussion was the facility in Wales again and they were holding a video-conference with the Welsh Environment Office to get an update on the raw sewage escaping into the sea.

It wasn't really anything the English Department for Water Supply and Sanitation would normally get involved in, but Amanda Trunnion insisted it was relevant to the work of the Commission, so they had to take part.

Also in the video-conference were Philip Knowles from the Environment Agency and Professor Potts in his capacity as Chief Environmental Officer to the Commission, joining from his chair by the open french windows, in his sunny study.

Amanda looked tired and fidgeted continually. When she spoke, it was only to open the meeting and request updates. Since then, she had been silent.

As the conversation began to run down however, she gathered herself and interrupting the technical bod at the English Environment Agency who was droning on about the rate at which solids broke down in fast flowing water and whether the size of the inflatable boom placed in the sea to try to contain the spill was sufficient, she spoke.

'This is turning into a talking shop,' she said controversially. 'It is not in my power to dictate how the Welsh teams organise themselves but, as of now, Patrick, I would like you to divide up the tasks the English are helping the Welsh with and set up a series of Working Groups who will report progress to you every couple of days. Once a week could you collate their reports, please, and circulate them. Right, I'm afraid you will have to excuse me, although by the look of things we are pretty well finished up here and I'm sure we all have plenty to do.'

And with that she got up and left the room, closely pursued by Patrick Blenny, of course.

As the senior officer left in the meeting, it fell to Tim to wrap up, thank everyone and, just in time to get to the sandwich shop, close the meeting down.

There was no time for Tim to return to his desk and brush his jacket with the old stiff brush he kept there, as he would normally do, and rather than wait for the lift he ran down the stairs.

The glorious sunny day which greeted him as he left the building made no impression on him, except to make him rather over-hot by the time he had bustled along to the sandwich shop.

As he burst through the door, he was just in time to see Hazel paying for her sandwich at the head of the lengthy queue.

Tim had to make a snap decision whether to join the other end of the line and wait, or forego his own sandwich and rush to Hazel's side.

'Oh hello, Tim,' smiled Hazel. 'I wasn't sure if you were coming today or I'd have saved you a place in the queue.'

'Thank you, but that isn't important, Hazel,' blustered Tim. 'What matters is are you all right now and over your hay-fever? I am most awfully sorry about the flowers setting you off, it was foolish of me not to ask if you were allergic to them.'

'Oh Tim, it was sweet of you to send them, and you weren't to know. I'm only sorry it ruined our date.'

Tim looked furtively around him, he did not want any colleagues from the office to hear their conversation or start rumours about him dating a journalist. Such things could be career defining in the Civil Service.

'Look, could we step outside, do you think?' said Tim, holding the door open.

Tim took Hazel's elbow and walked her swiftly around the corner to where the pavement was wider.

'Hey!' said Hazel, 'What's with the frog march?'

'Sorry, sorry. It's just that there were people in there from my office and I didn't want them to hear our conversation.'

'I see. Are you going to tell me some devastating Government secret about poison bugs in the water supply or something, then?'

'No .. I ...'

'It's all right. Relax. I realise I shouldn't have mentioned our relationship in there ... I'm sorry.'

'Relationship? Are we in a relationship, Hazel?'

'Would you like to be?'

'Yes please, if you would like that too.'

'Well, let's get this proper date back in the diary and we shall see what can be done,' smiled Hazel.

-ooOOoo-

In the corridor, on the way to the MP's entrance to the House of Commons chamber, Amanda encountered the Home Sec., Lakshmi Prakash, coming the other way surrounded by a cloud of flunkies.

'Excuse me, Home Secretary. Amanda Trunnion. I understand you wanted to see me about my Commission looking into …'

'I'm sorry, Amanda, I don't have time right now. Do you know Osbert's Club in Mayfair? Contact my PPS and arrange to meet me there after lunch for a coffee before the end of the week, please.' And with that she moved on.

Amanda had never heard of Osbert's Club, but she hastened to look up the number of Miss Prakash's Parliamentary Private Secretary and left him a message.

-ooOOoo-

'Bats, you say?' Kenneth Jones, the Welsh Senedd Minister, was taken aback. 'And you say this corporation that owns the mine are based in the British Virgin Islands and can't be contacted?'

'I'm afraid so, Minister,' said Gareth. 'The company effectively disappeared in 2007 when attempts were made to get them to properly restore land in compliance with the conditions of a Planning Permission on another mine they own. There has been no trace of them since. But it is the bats that may yet cause us a greater problem by here. If the word gets out that we intend to fill up their roost with human sh.. I mean excrement, the wildlife people will create merry hell for us.'

'Do we have any other options?'

'Just one, I'm told. There is the former quarry which was turned into a caravan holiday park many years ago. It is in a sort of basin with non-porous rock on three sides. The engineers say if they blocked off the fourth side with a wall they could pump thousands of gallons in there before it would affect the water table. It would only be a temporary solution, mind, and there would be a major cost to decontaminate and restore it when the plant itself was back up and running but …'

'And who owns this caravan site quarry place?'

'It is owned by an investment company, part of the merchant bank who also funded Bolas, the French contractor, alongside the EU, to pay for the construction of the bio-digester plant. They are headed by … you are not going to believe this … Sir Jacob Mortimer. He is the Chairman of the English Rural Infrastructure Environmental Commission, or 'RIEC 'for short, who as you know have just visited the site with that English Government Minister. Although I wouldn't be too surprised to find that he has no idea the caravan site forms part of the portfolio his investment company owns.'

'And there are no bats to worry about in this former quarry?'

'No bats, and after the explosion, no caravans.'

Kenneth Jones was struggling not to laugh out loud.

'Let me call my people about this and see what they think, and I'll get straight back to you,' he said.

-ooo0oo-

Amanda was too early, of course, and the Home Sec. was still dining, but the Concierge seemed to be expecting her and showed her through to the spacious bar area off the reception hall.

Osbert's Club was all rather grand and quite busy. As she looked around, she saw the former Prime Minister, Horace Smithson with a small group of smiling men and women laughing and drinking champagne in one corner, and in another, Simon Head, the one-time Deputy Leader of the House of Commons and fervent Brexit promoter, apparently on his own, nursing a large brandy.

Various waiters flitted to and fro. Some of the seats and tables were occupied by people she thought she recognised, but for the moment, and in her nervous state, she could not place them.

She found a seat and was immediately approached by a waiter who took her order for a black coffee.

She did not have long to wait until the Home Sec. herself emerged through some double doors and following directions from a tall thin bespectacled man at her side, moved towards her table.

Amanda stood up and shook hands.

'Amanda Trunnion,' she said. 'How do you do?'

'Quite well, thank you. But I'm afraid I can only spare you a couple of minutes, so can I start by saying that the Chief Whip has bought me up to speed on the project you are involved in and explained how you are going to help us promote our new green agenda with these bio-digester plants.'

'Yes, I ...'

'I hope he has also made it clear to you that you need to promote the idea of building more of these things, but drop the Brexit references and don't focus on the role of the EU in the existing Welsh one. All of that is bad news at the moment, and will take attention away from this green initiative, if we are not careful.'

'No, of course, I ...'

'Good, right. Can you let me have weekly written reports of progress please, and try to avoid upsetting the Welsh again.'

And with that, she turned on her heel and moved on to join

Horace Smithson and his cronies in the opposite corner.

Embarrassed, Amanda finished her coffee at a gulp, and made for the exit.

-ooo0oo-

FIFTEEN

The publication of the latest issue of 'The Gazette' caused quite a stir.

Hazel Trigg's in-depth account of the incident at the plant in Wales, with her 'before and after' photographs and balanced insights into what had happened at the site, as well as at the event afterwards, dealt with some of the more excitable reporting which had been splashed across the daily papers.

Hazel had written down the various headlines in her notebook as they appeared and whilst some made her shake her head in dismay at their inaccuracy, one or two made her laugh.

"Possible Terrorist attack at Government facility," touted The Daily Record.

"Huge explosion rips apart Welsh caravan site," stated The Telegraph.

"Failings in EU funded sewage scheme cause explosion," said the Daily Mail.

"French Contractor blamed for environmental disaster at EU flagship scheme," whispered The Financial Times, on an inside page.

"Sewage works blown up by gas leak," said the Welsh Times.

"*Enormous* EU sewage plant *explodes* in Wales," yelled The Evening Standard.

And best of all:-

"*EU covers Welsh in sh*t - literally!*" screamed The Sun.

Hazel's office advised her that early notifications of circulation figures for the latest edition of The Gazette were up by fifteen percent, as readers clamoured to read the detail of what happened.

-ooo0oo-

Piers Aubin was in the South of France with one of his footballer clients when Amanda Trunnion called him.

He had just finished arranging the sale of the reporting and photo rights for the huge wedding the footballer and his pop-singer/model fiancée planned in a couple of months time. He was very pleased with the lucrative deal he had struck, but somewhat concerned about the potential for the event being cancelled if the constant shouting matches and sniping remarks his client and fiancée were increasingly engaged in, could not be calmed down.

'I'm in a bit of a hole, Piers,' admitted Amanda. 'I need to put a bit of polish on things to impress the Home Sec. and get the Chief Whip to take his foot off my neck.'

'Tell me all about it,' said Piers, settling down to his second Mojito on the sun-lounger by the footballer's swimming pool.

-ooo0oo-

'That's right Potty,' said Sebastian Burleigh-Marks. 'And although I was not close enough to hear the actual conversation, she was giving the Trunnion woman quite a bollocking.'

'Thank you, Sebastian. That is very interesting. I have not met the new Home Secretary, do you know much about her?'

'Sour faced vicious little bully, just like the last one, by all accounts. One of the PM's recent intake of nasty yapping right-wingers.'

'Would you say she was not a keen supporter of the environment lobby, Sebastian?'

'She is too new for opinions to crystallise on that one. But the betting is strong that she will back any cause if it gathers in the popular vote.'

'Not much backbone, then?'

'None in evidence, so far at least. She is the PM's latest enforcer doing the dirtier work, as the role demands, but she does not seem to have any firmly held opinions of her own on anything much. She is a bit shouty, though, just like her predecessor.'

'Thank you, Sebastian. Your straight-forward word portraits are always very succinct. Keep up the good work!'

'Delighted, Potty, old man. We shall speak again anon.'

And with that the Professor ended the call and returned to planting out his lobelias.

-ooOoo-

Tim did not own a car, but he had been a member of the local 'car club' for several years.

He paid twelve pounds a month, which enabled him to use a car, if one was available. He could pick it up and return it to the designated store by the railway station, which was only a shortish walk from his house. It was no use on rail-strike days, of course, because it always got booked up long before he could get onto the 'app', but it was otherwise very easy to use.

Once a booking had been made, one simply approached the car, entered a code to unlock it and then a 'pin number' on the little key pad in the glove compartment, and the car would be ready to go.

Tim had used it a few times when he wanted to take stuff to the dump, or collect plants from a garden centre, or that sort of thing, although he did sometimes wonder if buying a car might actually turn out to be cheaper in the long run.

The first time he had used it was to pick up some flat pack furniture he'd ordered, and now he came to think about it, he had also used it to take the faulty chest of drawers back and get a replacement; and then again a year or so later to take the remains to the dump, when the dreadful thing finally fell to pieces.

Whichever way you looked at it, however, it was certainly cheaper than using taxis, and now Tim had an idea.

He looked on the website and discovered that a Vauxhall Corsa was available to hire on his chosen date. He had no idea whether a Vauxhall Corsa was a good car, but at least it wasn't a van or the more usually available small, square, basic Renault people carrier thing, which was really just a van with windows.

He wanted something presentable, not a utility vehicle, so he booked it and called Hazel.

'Are you free on Saturday?' he asked, and having established that she was, he gathered up his courage and said, 'How would you like to spend a day in the country with me?'

He went on to explain about the car club, the Vauxhall Corsa, and his idea to head out, perhaps towards Dorking, for lunch in a country pub.

'If you like I could pick you up at the station here and we could head off for a bit of fresh air.'

'I should like that very much, Tim,' said Hazel. 'Let me check out the train times and I'll get back to you.'

'Well, yes, but ...'

'But?'

'Well, afterwards, in the evening I mean, I could run you back up to London, so you don't have to travel alone.'

'Tim, that is very thoughtful and generous of you, but what if it gets late; don't you have to get the car back?'

'Oh, that's no problem. There was a special "two for one" offer on, so I've booked the car for the whole weekend.'

-ooOOoo-

The high-flying, high-cost, lawyer that Sir Jacob Mortimer always used for his banking activities got straight to the point.

The caravan site would have to be repaired before it could be brought back into use, but the operator who rented it was on a rolling monthly lease and might well decide to cut his losses and just walk away after the explosion did so much damage.

In any event the lease contained a 'break clause,' which enabled either party to cancel at short notice if the lease was breached, and the records showed that the caravan site operator was already a couple of months in arrears on the rent.

The lawyer went on to explain that, so long as a legally binding contract could be put in place to force the Welsh to clean up the site and restore it to its former state when it was no longer required, and if a suitably extortionate 'compensation package' could be agreed to pay for the use now proposed, it was no problem.

'Right,' said Sir Jacob. 'Serve the notice to sling the caravan chap off and think of a number, then double it, to put to the Welsh

Government people. As I understand it, they have run out of options as to what to do with the … the erm … waste until the main plant is repaired, so we have got them by the short and curlies.'

-ooOoo-

'I bet that wiped the smile off Kenneth Jones's face,' said the Home Secretary, taking another sip of her tea.

'It did rather,' said Sir Jacob Mortimer.

'Bloody Welsh, never liked them …' said former Prime Minister Horace Smithson, which caused giggling in the slightly inebriated group of people with him, in the bar at Osbert's Club in Mayfair.

'I must go,' Lakshmi Prakash was a busy woman and was due back in Westminster. 'If there is any backlash on us, I've lined up the Trunnion woman to take the fall, so it should do us no harm. Thanks for the tea, Horace.'

'Anytime, my dear,' said the former PM, looking her up and down appreciatively. 'Perhaps you and I should have lunch together. Privately, I mean, so I can get to know you better. Swap ideas and so forth …'

The Home Secretary smiled, but what she thought of that she kept to herself.

-ooOoo-

SIXTEEN

'You don't think they will make us redundant, do you Dai?' Ewan was beginning to worry about the time the clean-up operation and the repairs were taking.

'No, I don't think so Ewan. Nobody else knows how to operate the control centre by here like we do. I think we are safe enough.'

'I hope you are right, man. I've got a mortgage on my house and work round here is bloody scarce.'

'I suppose we could always ask to join the teams clearing up the muck?'

'No thank you.'

'No, you are right. Horrible job that is!'

-ooOOoo-

Morgan Evans surveyed the ruins with a shake of his head.

He was too old for this sort of thing he told himself, and the caravan site had been losing money for some time, so any insurance payout wasn't the only consideration.

Morgan had set up the campsite in the old quarry twenty years before, and added it to the list of small businesses he ran around and about the seaside town.

The little amusement arcade down by the beach that also sold inflatable beach toys and buckets and spades had made money. But now it was just a pile of rubble, and the beach was becoming so polluted that he doubted if the tourists would be coming back for a very long time, if ever.

His insurance claim was in, of course. But he had to be realistic about the time it might take to agree a payout. He knew he was in for a long wait.

Cash-flow is everything when you are well beyond retirement age and trying to keep a little empire of small enterprises together to top up your pension. But investment money to repair damage like this was not something Morgan could see himself being able to find. At his age nobody was going to lend him any money, especially to invest in businesses which had never really shown much of a profit in the first place.

Morgan lowered himself carefully and sat down on a charred but still serviceable camping chair, and laid his walking stick across his knees.

What he needed, he decided, was some money to fall from the heavens into his lap, and he decided that he must go to Chapel at the weekend and pray for something good to happen.

-oo0Ooo-

Amanda Trunnion sat alone in her office in Westminster.

There was quite an important debate going on in the Chamber, but it was late and she was tired, and tomorrow, being the second Saturday in the month, she had to be in her constituency to hold a 'surgery'.

She normally hated these 'meet the people' events and listening to the details of her constituent's neighbour disputes and complaints about the latest planning application. But this time

Piers Aubin had said he would see if he could arrange for a 'friendly' journalist to be there to ask pertinent questions about the work of the Commission, and the new 'green' plans, to make her look good.

After the disaster down in Wales, Piers had warned her to expect there to be several journalists at the locally well-publicised 'surgery' session, who might ask awkward questions. To be ready for that, he had worked with her to create a little 'crib sheet' of handy sound bites which could be used to turn the conversation into something positive.

She realised that what was about to happen would be bound to get back to the Home Secretary, even before she could write it up in her weekly report, so she was determined to be prepared.

-ooOOoo-

'Well, it will only take an hour or two, but the Editor insists,' Hazel had stated. 'The surgery starts at ten sharp, so I'll certainly be with you well before lunchtime,' Hazel said.

At ten to twelve, two hours after he had collected the Vauxhall Corsa, Tim was pacing around the garden looking for something to distract him.

He was ready to the last button for their day in the country, with all his plans carefully made, but Hazel's boss had disrupted the original timescale and Tim could not help feeling annoyed.

He checked that his mobile phone was turned on and not set to 'silent' once more, as he waited for Hazel to call him when she got to the station.

-ooOOoo-

'Oh, hello. Dewi Davis, isn't it ... from the Aberystwyth Advertiser?'

'Argus actually. Aberystwyth Argus. Hello again Hazel.'

'Sorry, yes, of course. You are bit off your home turf, aren't you?'

'Sort of a multi-tasking thing, actually,' said Dewi. 'I was due to come and see my sister and her kids who live not far from here, and knowing this is Amanda Trunnion's constituency, I looked up when she held her Saturday surgeries. Bit of luck actually.'

'I see. Very dedicated of you.'

'Well, see, our Minister is proper bent out of shape at the way the English Minister behaved down at the sewage place, so I thought I might see what she says about it here.'

'I see that we are not the only members of the Press in attendance. Look, there is a TV crew drawing up outside.'

'Blimey, I didn't expect that …'

'Neither did I. And there is Noel Grant, the anchor for 'Politics in Action' on GMTV. This is going to get interesting.'

-ooo0oo-

Inside now, with a cup of coffee, Tim turned on the TV and flicked through the channels to see if there was anything interesting in the news.

He spilled the hot coffee on his best trousers when Hazel came into view standing amongst a group of journalists behind a furious looking Amanda Trunnion, who was being interviewed, on the steps of what appeared to be a village hall, by Noel Grant, no less.

'So would you agree Minister,' he was saying, 'that this new, so-called green initiative to build more of these plants, is just political posturing if the EU funding that built the first one is not available?'

-ooo0oo-

SEVENTEEN

Professor Edwin Potts was almost ready to put his plan into action.

There were two plans, really. The first involved launching a fairly-detailed report on the 'best practice' to de-contaminate the plant in Wales and restore the damaged natural landscape around it.

The second was more political than practical and rather more confidential. Once the first plan was accepted by the English and Welsh Governments and underway, which would give credence and useful tangible outcomes to the work of the Commission, the second plan would mop up the political side of things and hopefully facilitate the delivery of what the professor's group ultimately desired.

As he put the finishing touches to the document containing the first proposal on his computer and pressed 'print', the Professor turned his mind to the question of pruning his apple trees, and he opened the french doors to the garden and looked up at the sky to gauge the weather and the likelihood of rain.

-ooOOoo-

It was almost two o'clock when, with his plans in tatters, Tim finally picked up Hazel from the railway station and put her little bag and her camera case in the boot. Any ideas of lunch in a country pub were now history.

Tim knew that, other than the burger places, the only restaurant likely to be still serving lunch was that little Italian on the High Street.

If Hazel was hungry, he explained, that was pretty much their only option, this late in the day.

'I'm sure it will be lovely,' Hazel said, and having found a space a few doors along they parked the car.

As the unmistakable and appetising Italian cooking smells enveloped them, Tim began to relax at last.

'It must have been a surprise when the TV people turned up,' commented Tim as their steaming bowls of pasta arrived.

'Certainly, and a nasty shock for Amanda Trunnion too. That Noel Grant tore her apart and left the pieces twitching on the ground.'

'What a nasty image as we are about to eat,' chortled Tim.

'Great copy for me though,' said Hazel twisting her fork expertly in the spaghetti. 'I'm sorry it all took so long, though. Have I spoilt all your plans?'

'No, not really, Hazel. I'm just glad we can be together.'

'That's sweet, Tim …'

'Yes, well. I thought this afternoon we could go down to a watermill I know near Dorking where they do watercress teas. Would you like that?'

'Near Dorking, you say? Lovely,' said Hazel. She did not let on that, although it was many years ago, she was pretty sure she had visited this very same watermill for a watercress tea with her first boyfriend.

'Right, so don't fill up on too much pasta and leave some room,' smiled Tim.

'Have you got any plans for tomorrow,' Hazel asked. 'Only seeing as you have the car for the whole weekend, and we lost this morning perhaps …'

'Damn it!' exclaimed Tim, and seeing Hazel's startled expression, explained his outburst. 'When that couple went out of the door just now, I noticed it was raining!'

'… Perhaps we could have the watercress tea tomorrow.'

'Pardon?' said Tim.

-ooOOoo-

'It wouldn't matter,' said Patrick Blenny to his wife, as they carried their lunch things in from the garden, as it started to rain. 'But she is so damn stupid. It's just like her to make those idiotic comments when cornered by the TV people, you could see it coming a mile off.'

Just as his wife told him for a second time that, whilst it was all very annoying, he should pick up the threads on Monday, but leave it for now, and try to enjoy his weekend, his mobile phone rang in his pocket.

'I need your help, Patrick,' said a very chastened Amanda Trunnion.

-ooOOoo-

'I'm sorry to call you on a Saturday, Professor, and I don't know if you are aware, but Amanda Trunnion has just made an idiot of herself on the TV news,' said Philip Knowles from the Environment Agency.

'How very unfortunate,' said the Professor, smiling to himself.

'Yes, well. I wondered how your plan for the environmental rescue and the restoration of the site down in Wales is coming along? If we could publish it now it would show the Commission in a good light and make sure that the rest of us are not made to look idiots too.'

'Fortunately, my little group have just completed the proposal, and we are about ready to present it to the two Governments for consideration. Would you like me to email you a copy?'

When the call finished and the email was sent, as it was now raining quite hard, Professor Potts retired to his greenhouse to attend to his lettuces. The apple trees would have to wait.

-oo0Ooo-

EIGHTEEN

'She has backed the Government into a corner, Potty,' said Sebastian Burleigh-Marks. 'At least that's what old Weasel-Face, I mean Hamish Glover, The Minister for the Environment and also minister of some other stuff that I have forgotten for the moment … Town Planning, was it? Regeneration? No, it's gone. Anyway, that's what he was saying. Strong words were being bandied about, and its a good job she was not present, because the Home Sec., who was supposed to be keeping an eye on the Trunnion, took some flack in absentia.'

'All very interesting,' said Professor Potts, smiling contentedly to himself.

'The PM is apparently hopping about in a rage, and the Chancellor is under pressure to come up with an allocation of funds. Weasel-Face, I mean Hamish Glover, is leading the charge on that and biting his ear for a big ring-fenced investment budget that they can announce to quell the rising alarm.'

'How exciting,' said the Professor.

'Horrid, I mean Horace Smithson thinks they will have to commit to an actual "programme" now, rather than just announcing another "initiative". Much harder to wriggle out of, a "programme" and all that sort of thing. He was a bit pissed when I spoke to him mind you, but that is nothing unusual since he started making good money by writing newspaper articles. Generally, though there is a fair amount of gloom and despondency and the feeling that messing about with green agendas is never a good idea for the Conservative Party.'

'Thank you, Sebastian. Excellent insights as ever. Keep up the good work!' smiled Professor Potts.

-ooo0oo-

When the lawyer offered him ten thousand pounds if he would forgo the one-month notice he was entitled to, and vacate the site immediately, Morgan Evans was overjoyed.

Almost before the transfer of funds to his bank was completed, several lorries loaded with what looked like giant red interlocking Lego bricks and rolls of plastic were arriving on the site.

Morgan had little interest in what they were doing as he collected a few potentially saleable items from the blackened remains on the site, but had he had stayed a little longer he would have seen a large hollow temporary wall being erected at considerable speed, and each of the red containers being filled with water before the next layer was fixed into place on top.

A thick sand layer was being spread out all over everything, and at least a dozen men were working at a frenzied pace on the project.

Other lorries were unloading huge roles of flexible pipe at the other end of the facility, near the still gushing broken pipeline.

While the drivers complained about the smell, the workers already on site, who mostly wore breathing apparatus, looked like spacemen directing operations.

Sir Jacob Mortimer smiled as he put his signature to the hastily drawn up agreement, which would see him collect a considerable sum from the Welsh Government for very little capital outlay, and virtually no work. That was just the sort of business he liked doing best.

-ooOOoo-

'This is more like it,' said Dai. 'Some action at last.'

'The speed that dirty great red wall is going up by here! That's really clever, that is,' Ewan was impressed.

'And they are laying half a dozen new pipes to it from over that side,' observed Dai. 'I wouldn't be surprised if they can't start pumping into that thing in a day or so.'

'Have you seen how full the overflow tank is getting? They need that new thing up and running as soon as possible if you ask me.'

'Too right. They are still taking broken bits off the damaged silo and the turbine, mind. Looks like it is going to be some time before they will be putting it back together and getting it back into action.'

'Here, two across ...' said Ewan, picking up his paper and showing Dai the crossword. 'Any ideas?'

-ooOOoo-

'So, you don't want me to run you back there tonight, Hazel?'

'No, there seems no point. It occurs to me that if I could stay down here, we could take our trip out into the countryside in the morning, if it has stopped raining by then.'

'Erm ... I see what you mean ... But ...'

'If you like I could book into a hotel tonight ...' Hazel flashed Tim a mischievous grin.

'Oh, there is no need to do that, Hazel. You could stay in my house for the night ...'

'Are you proposing that I spend the night, unchaperoned, under your roof, Mr. Blande? What about my reputation!' teased Hazel.

'Well, I didn't mean to presume ... I just thought that from a practical point of view ...'

'I'm just kidding, Tim. I would love to stay in your house, assuming you don't have hoards of housemates all clamouring for the bathroom.'

'No, I live alone, Hazel. I thought you knew that.'

'So you are inviting me into your bachelor pad, are you? Very forward of you, I must say!'

'Well ...'

'Lighten up Tim. I will be delighted to come to your house and, if you treat me to a light supper beforehand, who knows what may follow. Would you like that?'

'Hazel, I would love it.'

-ooOoo-

NINETEEN

Sunday dawned bright and clear, with no sign of yesterday's heavy rain.

The apple trees were still too wet to prune and might be a bit slippery, the Professor thought, so he decided to examine his bee hives instead and then make the preparations for his Sunday lunch.

He had taken another call from Philip Knowles quite late the previous night and was gratified that Philip, and his Environment Agency colleagues, seemed very happy with the proposal he had emailed over. He expected, now that was done, that his Sunday would be undisturbed.

Plenty of time next week, he thought, to start the preparations required for his other plan; and he smiled happily as he pulled on his bee-keeper's gown and stepped into his over-sized wellington boots.

-oooOoo-

What had possessed him to change his sheets on Saturday morning, Tim had no idea, but he was glad he did. His normal modus-operandi was to change them and put them in the washing machine on a Sunday night.

The newish towels were also laid out in the bathroom, which was just the way the rota of washing these things turned out. Tim's strict programme of when to wash what, was designed for his ease and convenience and had nothing to do with Hazel coming to stay; which it must be said, was completely unplanned, after all.

It was just a coincidence that the clean bedding and the fluffiest towels became available at the same time as her visit.

Tim and Hazel went back to bed twice before they got up, and now with the clock rapidly approaching ten o'clock, hunger and the need for coffee eventually drove them to get out of bed.

'I think,' said Hazel, as she sipped her coffee sitting on the side of the bed, 'that that is the worst night's sleep I have ever had ... and I'm really pleased about that!'

'I think,' chortled Tim, 'that you are the randiest journalist I have ever met, Hazel.'

'Oh yes?' said Hazel. 'And how many other journalists have you dragged back here to your den and had your wicked way with?'

'Dozens,' lied Tim. 'But there's only one I want to do it with again, right now!'

Eventually, at a little after noon, when they awoke from a fitful slumber, Tim and Hazel shared a bath, and then finally they got dressed.

'There is just time to drive down to Dorking for that watercress tea,' announced Tim.

'Can I be honest,' said Hazel. 'I hate watercress. Can't we just go to a nice pub for a quiet lunch?'

'On the strict understanding that we come back here afterwards before I have to take you back to London, I agree,' said Tim.

'Why might you want to come back here first, Timothy?' asked Hazel, fluttering her eyelashes.

'Because they don't have any beds in the saloon bar of the Horse and Groom, and after a solid Sunday roast I shall have need of one.'

'You will get no sleep at all, you know,' smiled Hazel.

'That is rather what I was hoping,' laughed Tim.

-ooOOoo-

Although it was a Sunday, the pace of work on the site in Wales did not slacken at all.

The enormous red plastic block wall was nearing completion by late afternoon, and would have been further advanced if the contractors could encourage the water from the hoses to run into the enormous interlocking hollow blocks a little faster.

The vast cavern they had created, now lined with layers of black rubberised plastic, thicker than, but basically of the same sort used to line garden ponds, was almost ready to go.

What was left of Nigel and Alison's car and the few tiny parts remaining of their uninsured caravan now lay under a thick layer of sand hastily dug up and transported from the beach, covered by the substantial plastic liner.

Morgan Evans, looking at it now with a scarf around his face to mitigate the smell as he took a walk after his Sunday lunch, shook his head in disbelief.

Maybe, he thought, he should have held out for a bigger payment. But a little voice in his head told him that he had been very lucky, and just to be grateful for what he had got.

He resolved, having missed it this morning, that he would go to Chapel this evening, and give thanks for the miracle that had been bestowed upon him.

-ooOOoo-

'The mood in Osbert's Club was initially rather gloomy, but since then a certain muted buoyancy has returned.'

'I'm glad to hear that, Sebastian. Happy politicians make better decisions.'

'Let's hope you are right, Potty, old man. I've set up a little luncheon party and invited Weasel-Face, I mean Hamish Glover, along as you suggested, but I wonder if you could just remind me again of what I am supposed to be helping him to come to terms with? A quick flick through the diaries I kept when we were at Oxford together has given me the reference point I require. I was reminded of a certain rather juicy incident involving his parents visiting college in an attempt to deflect any unpleasantness after Hamish, wearing his kilt, did something injudicious involving 'Oxford Union' branded underpants … but before I go into bat, I want to be sure I have completely understood the outcome you desire.'

'You would like me to go through it again, Sebastian?'

'Yes, please, Potty old man. You see I was still somewhat polluted from a rather excitable champagne reception when we spoke last, and I had not actually had terribly much sleep, so the finer points of your words rather slipped away from me. Sorry, and so on and so forth.'

'Well, try to stay sober when you put the case to Hamish Glover, Sebastian, if you wouldn't mind.'

'Oh of course, absolutely. Won't happen again, Professor. Now, say on … I'm all ears.'

BOBABLE

-ooOoo-

TWENTY

'This is very timely,' said Sir Jacob Mortimer, speaking in his capacity as chairman of the Commission. 'I want to publish this now so that it will take some of the attention away from Amanda's unfortunate interview on TV.'

The Cabinet Minister he was addressing nodded and turned to speak to the PM who was sitting beside him in the Cabinet Room in 10 Downing Street. He muted the microphone before he spoke, so that Sir Jacob, sitting at his desk in Holborn would not hear what he was saying.

He was not left holding on for long, and when the microphone was turned back on he could hear the PM shouting in the background, as in two words the Minister told him to go ahead, and then cut the conference call connection.

Sir Jacob smiled in relief. At least, with the report to hide behind, as the PM inevitably sacked and washed his hands of Amanda Trunnion, none of the mud would stick to him.

He started to dial Piers Aubin's number, and he realised that, as soon as Piers got it out to the press, the Welsh Government would also be forced to publicly endorse it, to save face.

He must remember to thank Professor Potts personally for

his work producing the decontamination and recovery plan so quickly.

-ooOoo-

'So, after that,' Philip Knowles explained, 'once my opposite number in the Welsh Environment Agency office accepted it, Sir Jacob took it up the line and the Press are being briefed as we speak.'

'That is excellent news, Philip,' said Professor Potts, buttering a piece of toast. 'A good result all round.'

Before he ended the call, Philip paid the Professor a personal tribute.

'Thank you, Professor. Without you this could not have happened.'

-ooOoo-

Tim was sitting at one of the little tables in the sandwich shop, when Hazel arrived.

'So there is going to be another press conference about the plan to deal with the environmental disaster at the plant in Wales this afternoon, with a live-link to the Welsh Government offices,' Hazel explained. 'They will stage it in the Queen Elizabeth Hall because it is going to get such a lot of Press interest.'

'All we have been told so far is that you-know-who is on garden leave and to await further news.'

'Has she been sacked already then?'

'A weekend is a long time in politics,' smiled Tim.

-ooOoo-

'So, Weasel-Face, I mean Hamish Glover has agreed with the PM to work with land owners to find suitable sites to build these things on.'

'I thought he might be chosen for that task, Sebastian. He is the Town Planning Minister, is he not?'

'Yes, Professor, along with Environment and Regeneration. His Ministry has been expanded continually in recent months, until he seems to be in charge of almost everything.'

'Heaven forbid, given what you have told me about him. But what is the view from the Treasury? Has the Chancellor done anything about finding the money yet?'

'Hard to say, Potty, old man. Hard to say. The betting here is that the PM has sat on him hard and now it is all but inevitable that they are not going to get away with just another "initiative". The obvious first question is where the money is coming from if this has to become a proper "programme"'.

'I see.'

'Some of the left wingers are saying it is becoming unstoppable and that we might have to actually build some of the bally things if the Conservatives are to hang onto power after the next election.'

'Fascinating. And thank you Sebastian, this is certainly getting interesting'

-oooOoo-

Bio-Power Solutions (Oxford) Ltd. held its first board meeting to agree the official 'Memorandum and Articles' of the new company.

It was decided that Steven (call me Steve) Browning would be the Chairman and Anne Pickles would be the Managing Director, and as that concluded the business on the Agenda, the meeting was closed.

'Right, we both need to sign,' said Anne. 'And then I must dash, or I will be late for my lecture.'

'OK, sweetheart. See you at home tonight,' smiled Steve, and adjusted his cycle helmet and brushed the last traces of flour from his jacket before mounting his bicycle, which was leaning by the back door of Browning's Artisan Bakery, where he worked for his father in the family business.

-ooOoo-

'So, if the Home Sec. will accept this, do you think it is ready to submit now, Piers?'

Amanda Trunnion had been working on her Ministerial resignation letter with Piers Aubin.

The Home Secretary had told her she must produce it by lunchtime so that it could be released to the Press in time to catch the TV news and be discussed on the various politics programmes due to air then.

I was not an easy thing to do, and Amanda was glad that Piers still seemed to be on her side.

'And you really think I should put in that bit that goes "I am still convinced that the Government plan to build a range of these facilities across the Country is prudent and sensible, and I regret that I was not aware that the proposal for funding this programme was already under scrutiny in your office when I made my statement to the press".

You know that is not true, don't you, Piers? The Government hadn't even talked about really building any more of these things, let alone putting public money into them when all this happened.'

'Yes, I realise that,' said Piers. 'But when you told that reporter that the Government would fund them through taxes, when he pushed you about what could replace the EU funding used in the Welsh one, they couldn't say they didn't really intend to build any more of the things anyway, and it was all just talk to bolster their fake green agenda.'

'No, I know that was a mistake and I should never have said it, but that Noel Grant just wouldn't stop hectoring me about it and I felt I had to say something …'.

'Yes. It was a pity that the Leader of The Opposition picked up on that so quickly and started shouting about more Tory stealth taxes and so on. That rather backed the Home Sec. into a corner'.

'She could have denied the whole thing, miserable little pipsqueak. She didn't have to chuck all her toys out of the pram and make this happen'.

'It seems to me that is typical Number 10 style politics for you, Amanda. All very brutal'.

-ooOOoo-

'So, Sir Jacob, this morning Hamish Glover told me in clear terms that he will arrange for our three biggest town planning applications to be approved, if we go with this idea', said Jeff Bishop, the Chief Executive of Diospyros Developments. 'That is over sixteen thousand houses, and some of that land has been tied up in planning appeals for over ten years.'

'And this includes the new town you proposed near Swansea, does it Jeff?'

'Yes, and if your finance consortium is still interested, we can get heads of terms for a funding agreement written up as soon as you like.'

'Well, that is very good news. Just one thing, though,' Sir Jacob Mortimer was always careful to get the detail right, 'you are splitting this with other house builders, aren't you?'

'Oh yes, don't worry about that. Diospyros might be the largest property developer in the country, but that project is too big even for us. We have a consortium of eight major house builders lined up on that one, although we will provide all the infrastructure, the roads and so-on for it, and keep a chunk to develop ourselves under the Pomegranate Homes banner, of course.'

'Of course. When would you like to meet my colleagues to start looking at this, Jeff?'

'Would next week be too soon?'

-ooOOoo-

TWENTY-ONE

'So, you see there is no impact on the Public Purse and the occupants of the new homes will be getting almost free, completely green electricity,' Hamish Glover held his audience on the weekly television politics programme spellbound. 'The country will be getting badly needed new homes, the developer's land-banks will be built on at last, and the strain on public infrastructure, in terms of drainage and electricity, will be minimal. The owners of the new homes might even be able to export some electricity to the National Grid. That is more than a 'win-win' situation. In fact, I have lost count of how many wins that is!'

'But will these houses have to have a huge bio-digester like the one that blew up in Wales in their back gardens?' asked the presenter.

'A miniaturised and much improved version of that. Not much like the Welsh one at all, actually, and much more efficient. And not in their back gardens, no. They will probably be mostly underground, perhaps in the public open spaces that will need to be provided as part of the Planning requirements.'

'What about the danger of these things blowing up?' asked a particularly awkward Opposition MP.

'These are very much more advanced than the Welsh system, and they won't be built by French contractors under an EU lowest price tender arrangement, either. The proposal is that a British company, created for the purpose, manages and oversees their manufacture and installation, and the whole process is funded by the house-builders.'

-ooOOoo-

'Did you see it, Professor? Hamish Glover was on one channel, and Lakshmi Prakash was on the other side, both saying the project has the green light!'

'I rarely watch television, Anne, but I did watch some of that. Very encouraging, I thought.'

'It's wonderful, Professor,' said Steve Browning, smiling into the FaceTime screen. 'You have pulled off a miracle!'

'Oh now, I wouldn't go that far. Just a little nudge in the right direction here and there, that is all that was needed.'

'You are a wonder, Professor Potts,' smiled Anne, 'I always said so.'

'My dear, you are much too kind ...'

'Do you really think we will pull it off?'

'I have no idea, but if you play your part, and barring any unforeseen difficulties, we may yet achieve our aims.'

-ooOOoo-

Watching the news and re-runs of the earlier politics programmes when he got home that night, Tim was impressed.

When Hazel phoned, and they discussed the media event at the Queen Elizabeth Hall, he explained what he had seen.

'Somehow or other, I get the impression that this is being very carefully orchestrated,' he said. 'By whom and for what purpose I have no idea. Do you get that feeling, Hazel?'

'It is as clear as the nose on your face, Tim,' said Hazel. 'When Amanda Trunnion, who was clearly right out of her depth, landed the Government in an awkward spot, they either had to deny it all, or back the programme. Denying it would have exposed that their 'green agenda' was just so much talk, and backing it would have had a cost for the Chancellor. However, they reached quite a neat compromise by pushing it off on the house builders in return for giving them Planning Consent on some of the land they have been fighting to develop for years. Very clever.'

'But none of these miniaturised versions of the Welsh plant they were talking about exist as far as I can find out. What do you think is going on here, Hazel?'

'I suspect that a bit of cleverness will emerge shortly. Whoever is masterminding this will probably present the Government with some system that they have developed and, with no other option, the Government will have to grab it with both hands and back it, which will give the people behind it the credibility to develop their system and get investors to put up the necessary capital to turn it into reality.'

Tim smiled to himself at how well Hazel had pieced it all together.

'I would not be surprised,' he said, 'if it turns out that this is some huge but well-connected corporation trying to push their invention.'

-ooo0oo-

Bio-Power Solutions (Oxford) Ltd., was certainly not a huge corporation. It was actually one undergraduate working her way through university in Oxford, and a Masters Graduate from the same institution who was somewhat uncertain about which direction his career may take in the future. But they had the advantage of one or two very good connections of their own, and a viable and working miniature bio-digester and gas-powered turbine.

As Tim and Hazel were discussing the news, the two Executive Directors of the newly formed company were helping Professor Edwin Potts to prune his apple trees, and when that was done the next item on the agenda was to take the Professor out for a pizza.

-ooOoo-

TWENTY-TWO

The smaller of the three modern blocks of student living accommodation on campus at St John's College in Oxford, where the experimental miniature bio-digester and gas turbine had been installed, was the home of Wally Walters, a post graduate student with a first class degree in mechanical and fluid engineering. He, and a handful of undergraduates had built the system themselves, and it had performed faultlessly ever since.

Now with interest from Ceylex Engineering in mass-producing the pressurised mini-silo and the gas turbine unit, alongside Balance Electrical Systems involvement in production of the wiring, controls and software as used on the initial project, the mini bio-digester and gas turbine was a viable manufacturing proposition.

Steve Browning and Anne Pickles lived in a little rented flat over a hairdresser's shop about a mile and a half from the bakery where Steve worked, and about three quarters of a mile from the college where they met, and where their best friend Wally lived on the campus.

Anne was also at the college, in her final year of a business studies and accountancy degree and was expected to excel at whatever she turned her hand to. Steve had worked for a major engineering firm while he did his Master's degree, but now worked in his father's bakery while he "considered his options".

All three had studied under Professor Edwin Potts before he retired and along with a small group of his former students, all talented graduates and undergraduates, and a couple of other college lecturers, they now formed a little band of clever and resourceful people who worked together on diverse projects from time to time.

Professor Potts had awoken in each of the young people a strong sense of citizenship and the desire to use their talents to improve life for others as much as for themselves. They all saw value in protecting and enhancing the natural environment and several had gone on to work in public service in one form or another.

The main thing which kept them all together, though, was a huge respect for Professor Potts as a thinker as much as a teacher, mentor and guide. They were all devoted to him and would always be willing to help him in any way they could.

One of this group was not so young and she was telephoning the Professor now.

'Hello Edwin, I am just calling to congratulate you. The news coverage was very interesting.'

'Misato! How very pleasant to hear from you, and unless I am mistaken, all the way from Seattle.'

'You are correct, of course, but not for much longer,' said Misato. 'I am now returning to St John's to take up a new post next year, so I will be on the spot to watch how things develop.'

Since leading the team which invented and then refined the process used in the bio-digesters, Japanese-born Professor Misato Ho had been tempted away to an American university, but she had always considered Oxford as her home and she was pleased to be returning to end her career there, for the handful of years before she too retired.

'Congratulations are due to you too then, Misato. The Physics Faculty will be greatly enhanced with you as its new head.'

'How did you know about that post becoming vacant?'

'Oh, you know, word gets around,' smiled Professor Potts, putting down his secateurs and standing back to admire his neatly trimmed apple trees. 'Can you resend that recipe for apple sauce you gave me, I appear to have mislaid it'.

-ooo0oo-

'It's all complete apple sauce, as they say in America,' said Misato. 'The UK Government doesn't know if it's on its elbow or arsehole, as usual!'

Misato had been reading the Government's press releases about the proposed new bio-digester and gas turbine plants.

'Wally is a genius and his system has been working a treat after two, or is it three years, but it is not yet tried in a commercial or, for that matter, big residential setting. It's a big gamble, Professor. Are you sure it's going to be all right?'

'My friends will be encouraging Hamish Glover, the Government Minister in charge, to set up five or six demonstration projects on housing developments currently being built, Misato. The idea is to choose sites which are already capable of being connected to the live drainage system. Thereby, if it goes wrong, they can simply switch back to the original gravity sewage system. But if it proves reliable and generates a good amount of free electricity to power the homes, the residents will love it and the Government and the housing developers will be encouraged to roll it out far and wide.'

'But can it be manufactured in the volumes required?'

'Our young friends are confident that the arrangements they have in place now will be sufficient to guarantee supply in the short term, and thereafter the idea is to license the system to other manufacturing companies and collect royalties each time the system is installed.'

'Seems like you've got the bases covered, Professor!'

'Oh no, not me ... this is all the work of our young entrepreneurs and scientists. My role is insignificant.'

'More apple sauce, Professor! Just remember you can't kid an old physicist like me!'

'I wouldn't dream ...'

'No, but the funny stuff aside, this is a great opportunity and I hope our young friends all appreciate how clever you are at making things happen, and how lucky they are to be associated with you. I wish you all the very best of luck and if there is anything I can do to help, you only have to ask.'

-oo0Ooo-

Yet another train strike had been announced and Tim had to think about his contingency plans.

Several of his colleagues decided, once more, to take the day off rather than risk taking on the alternative methods of getting to work, such as they were. But although he had plenty of leave left to take, Tim wanted to get into town to see Hazel in the sandwich shop if he could.

He had just made up his mind to chance his luck by using a series of buses to brave the journey in, when his mobile phone buzzed and he noticed a text from Hazel.

'Got an idea for the day after tomorrow when this train strike is on. Please call me when you are able to discuss.'

Tim pocketed his phone and headed to the toilets where he hoped he could call without being disturbed.

'The thing is,' Hazel was saying, when the call connected, 'you could stay with me in London, while this train strike is on, I mean.'

'Really?' said Tim.

'So what I thought was … if you are interested and could swing it … and if you came over the night before … tomorrow night, I mean … We could spend the evening together and maybe go out for dinner or something.'

'Well, that would be lovely,' said Tim.

'The sofa bed in my studio flat makes up into a king size double and is really quite comfortable …'

'You really do come up with the most tempting ideas, Hazel.'

'I know,' giggled Hazel. 'Aren't you lucky!'

TWENTY-THREE

When Tim got back to his desk, Patrick Blenny was bustling into the department ahead of a thin man, who seemed to be all ears and feet with a vacant expression on his face, who was trying to keep up.

'Ah Tim, there you are. Can I introduce Gordon Sparrow, our new Minister. Gordon is the MP for Northeast Norfolk and was appointed as our Minister last night.'

'How do you do,' said Tim and shook the new Minister's limp hand.

'Er … yes,' said the Minister.

'Tim is my number two and can deputise for me on any issue,' Patrick was saying.

In a Government department focussed on sewage management, being referred to as a 'number two' was never something Tim relished. If he was ever promoted to take over Patrick's job, he would ban the expression he vowed.

'Very good. Very good …' said the new Minister. 'We will have to have lunch one of these days, I'm very new to all this, you see, and could do with all the guidance I can get.'

'Yes, well,' said Patrick, mortified. 'We can always make a meeting room available for you here, Minister, of course, but normally entertaining the staff is not necessary.'

'Oh, ah … Sorry. As I said, much to learn, much to learn.'

As Patrick hurried his new boss away to meet more of the staff, Tim shrugged. This one couldn't be any worse than the last one, he hoped.

-oo0Ooo-

Anne Pickles was struggling to get the freshly copied and bound documents she had just collected from the printers more safely secured in the basket on the front of her bicycle.

The panniers over the back wheel were already bulging with all the copies she could fit in, and there was a heavy cardboard boxful tied to the rack above them. With no more room, the basket would have to carry the last few. This basket, mounted on the handlebars was not really designed to hold thick printed documents with comb binders and slippery plastic cover pages, and all the weight caused the bicycle to wobble alarmingly.

She readjusted the stretchy elastic straps at the traffic lights, and as they turned green, did her best to make progress without losing any of the precious cargo.

Thank goodness Steve was going to borrow his father's van to take them to the post office, once they had got them all into the individual envelopes with the covering letters, she thought.

When the documents hit the desks of the various experts, academics, politicians and financiers, they needed to be in pristine condition and hopefully not suffering any signs of a fall from her bicycle as she took them home.

After another wobble round a pothole, Anne stopped and dismounted. It would be safer to walk the bicycle with its precious cargo the rest of the way, she decided.

-ooOOoo-

'His name is Gordon Sparrow, Potty. He went to Winchester College with the PM and then Cambridge, so I've not really had much to do with him. I did go to school with his older brother, but he went into pharmaceuticals, I think it was, so we lost touch.'

'I see, Sebastian. So what do we know about this Gordon Sparrow?'

'Bit of a chinless wonder, by all accounts. Lived in the family pile in darkest Norfolk and managed the estates there before going into politics, apparently. Got himself into a bit of a tangle with a local girl at one point, but that blew over with no harm done. Other than that, he is not much of a clubman and prefers books to bookmakers so is not seen on the turf or at any of the regular haunts.'

'A quiet man who keeps himself to himself then?'

'Well, there is just one thing. Apparently, he likes to sail and keeps quite a smart boat off the coast somewhere in Norfolk. He took himself off for three months in it once a few years ago. That was after the local girl incident. Now he likes to take it out at the weekend if he can.'

'Thank you, Sebastian. I'm sure all that will come in handy at some point. Keep up the good work!'

-ooOOoo-

Wally Walters was waiting outside her flat in his wheelchair when Anne arrived, and he helped her to unload the precious documents from the bicycle and carried them on his lap into the hall, where they were stacked on the stairs.

As she tucked her bicycle in its little spot beneath the staircase, leaving just enough room for Wally's wheelchair, she thanked him and asked if he fancied a cup of tea.

'That would be great,' said Wally, and began hauling himself up the stairs using his arms and both hands on the stair rail. 'And then before we make a start on this lot, perhaps we could go through the latest data print-out from the turbine. I think you will find the figures encouraging.'

'Right-ho, Wally,' said Anne, bringing the first pile of documents up the stairs behind him and positioning them on the dining table, prior to putting the kettle on. 'And then I've got to print off all the individual letters and the address labels.'

'Can I be doing that while you bring the rest up the stairs?'

'No, you make the tea,' smiled Anne, setting off to collect another pile, 'I'll soon have these upstairs and I'll be ready for some tea after that.'

While the kettle boiled, Wally had picked up one of the fat documents and was reading the first couple of pages as he propped himself against the kitchen units.

'Professor Potts's introduction is masterful, isn't it. Even on second reading it makes a really strong case. I'd be surprised if everyone who gets one of these isn't clamouring to get on board by the end of next week.'

-ooOoo-

'Well, you do have to take your hat off to those guys,' said Dai. 'I was amazed at how quick that temporary wall went up, and as soon as they have netting across it to keep the birds off, they are ready to turn on the pumps.'

'Fantastic,' said Ewan. 'I only wish they would hurry up and get the turbine fixed as well.'

'It is not surprising that is taking a while, though,' said Dai, putting the completed crossword down on the console where Ewan worked. 'That pipe tore a hole about twenty-five feet long in the side of the silo and then the gas blew out all the gubbins inside taking out almost a third of the turbine wall. That is a lot of damage to repair.'

'Oh, Dai! You have finished the whole thing,' complained Ewan, picking up the crossword puzzle. 'I only wanted your help with a couple of clues!'

-oo0Ooo-

It felt odd travelling to work on the train with a suitcase.

Tim remembered family holidays in his youth when his parents would take him, and copious amounts of luggage, on long train journeys to stay, self-catering, in places as diverse as Cornwall and Norfolk as he grew up.

But then the trains were half empty, and the commuter crush he was experiencing now was made all the more uncomfortable by having the case to contend with.

What did encourage him however, was the thought of what lay ahead at the end of his journey. An evening with Hazel and then staying in her little flat was an enticing prospect.

He stood now with his suitcase between his legs, holding onto one of the straps dangling from the roof of the tube train, and pressed up against his fellow passengers. He was hemmed in by a rotund woman dressed in sombre black holding a briefcase, a builder with a large tool bag and several suited businessmen, all struggling to stay on their feet as the train hurtled through the tunnels. As usual nobody was talking, and most of those lucky enough to find a seat had their noses buried in the morning newspapers, or scrolled through the news feeds on their mobile phones.

Living in the suburbs had its compensations, but the crush of the daily commute was certainly not one of them, and he envied Hazel her 'work from home' location just around the corner from Whitehall.

-oooOoo-

As Steve finished unloading the van at the parcel office and placed his hands on his back as he straightened up, one of the postmen, leaving the premises with a full trolley smiled at him and said,
'You should try doing this for a living and heaving that sort of thing about day after day. Much easier just delivering a few loaves of bread, I'd say!'

For a moment Steve was not sure what he meant, but then he realised that seeing the words Browning's Artisan Bakery emblazoned on each side of the little van might lead anyone to expect him to be a baker's roundsman. An easy mistake to make.

-oooOoo-

TWENTY-FOUR

First thing, Gordon Sparrow had a somewhat embarrassing meeting with Amanda Trunnion, during which she handed over the details of the 'Commission' which, of course, he would now be heading up.

He appreciated the delicacy of the situation and felt for the poor woman as she prepared to return to the backbenches and political obscurity. His own elevation had been a considerable surprise, and he found himself wondering if he was going to suffer the same ignominious fate as Amanda Trunnion if he made a mistake.

Fortunately, this Patrick Blenny fellow seemed to have matters in hand, although he suspected that his 'number two', Tim something-or-other, did the real work and was the backbone of this little team.

As soon as the meeting was over, he got on with arranging a few personal effects in the office, or rather half an office, which Ms. Trunnion had just vacated.

Now on his own, he unpacked and applied sticky fixers to the four corners of a bright framed photograph and after deciding on the best position, put it on the wall.

He suspected that his visits to "Morning Mist" would be more infrequent now, but at least he would have this picture of his cherished yacht to look at, as he toiled away in this cramped little office.

-ooOoo-

Professor Potts was disappointed with his apple trees.

Now that the spindly branches were trimmed back and the potential crop could be seen, there did not seem to be as much of it as at this time last year. The weather was having an effect, of course, and it had changed so much in recent years. The Professor sighed at the inevitability of it all.

He wandered over to his vegetable plot and glanced at the recently planted out carrots and onions. At least they seemed sturdy enough. Perhaps the apple trees would do a little better without those extraneous branches to support, he thought.

Out of the corner of his eye he saw the postman making his way up the drive towards the front door carrying what looked like a heavy parcel, so he made haste indoors to relieve the honest chap of his burden.

-ooOoo-

'Manna from bloody Heaven!' said Hamish Glover, putting aside the substantial document he had just read. 'Get that Gordon Sparrow twerp on the line, would you Emma …' he called, 'I've got a job for him to do.'

-ooOoo-

After he circulated copies of the document, Sir Barton Parish and some of his more senior Highways Agency people who had been told to read it, came together in the meeting room down the corridor.

'Right, look,' said Sir Barton, turning his hearing aid up a notch and tapping the fat document in front of him. 'This is all pretty clever stuff, and you might wonder how it affects us in Highways, so allow me to enlighten you.'

Sir Barton looked around the room to make sure he had the full attention of all his underlings.

'The Government have decided to rush through planning approvals on a range of major developments which have been on the cards, in some cases, for many years. Some of those developments have been held up on Highway grounds amongst other things, and once the list is circulated later this morning, I want you each to go through it and see which ones we have objected to and why.'

Sir Barton tapped the document in front of him again and continued.

'Then you are to make suggestions as to how our objections might be resolved or removed and let me have a full breakdown by the end of the week. I warn you that we are being told by Government that they will take a very dim view if we don't come up with positive solutions, and we must be prepared to break new ground with innovative ways to solve problems and be less prescriptive than ... than perhaps we would normally be ... in helping these projects along.'

Sir Barton looked around the room at the astonished faces of his most senior officers. This reversal of the established modus operandi of the department had shocked them all.

'I will personally sign off each of the positive solutions you come up with that will remove our current objections ... and I shall want to know the reason why we are still holding up any projects where you cannot find a way to resolve the problems or make suggestions in a pro-active way.'

He picked up the document and stood as he prepared to leave the room.

'I realise that this will come as something as a shock to many of you, and this is certainly going to be a new way of working for us all, but I am assured that if we can satisfy our political masters on this, the next round of pay talks will be … erm, less of a battle for us. Right, you all know what to do … let's crack on!'

-oo0Ooo-

TWENTY-FIVE

Next up, Gordon Sparrow had to go over to the Home Office with Patrick Blenny and Tim whatever-his-name-is for a meeting with some people from the National Grid and the Home Sec., Lakshmi Prakash herself.

Gordon had never met the Home Sec., and realised he must do his best to make a good impression.

He knew the meeting was something to do with that great big document that had arrived, but although he had read some of it, he could not imagine what.

Shrugging into his suit jacket, he thought all would become clear soon enough. He might have been rather bemused at the pace at which things moved, now that he was a Minister, but he was determined to do his level best to keep up.

With a last glance at the image of "Morning Mist" in its frame on the wall, he closed the office door and tried to remember which way he needed to turn to get to the exit.

-oo0Ooo-

With his overnight case tucked discreetly underneath his desk Tim was surprised to see how empty the department was.

With the imminent train strike, several of his colleagues had taken holiday, of course, and some had arrived very late for work as the first rumblings from the picket lines began to have an effect, and the rail network began to be disrupted.

Somehow Patrick had managed to get in which, considering that he lived somewhere out in Essex, was a surprise. Although, as they left for the Home Office, he explained that in the end his wife had driven him as far as the outskirts of the City, so that he only had a tube journey to contend with. Getting home tonight might not be so simple, he had said.

When they arrived at the Home Office they were shown through to a meeting room and found Gordon Sparrow already there.

He had just introduced himself to the head of UK Power Networks and was shaking hands with the Chief Executive of the National Grid, and his Executive Assistant, when the door burst open and the Home Sec., Lakshmi Prakash, and a tall man with spectacles joined the meeting.

After the introductions, during which those present learned that the tall man was Austin Hogg-Wright, who announced rather grandly, in a plummy public school accent, that he had the "privilege of being Private Secretary to Ms.Prakash", the meeting got underway.

'Not to put too fine a point on it,' the Home Secretary stated, 'the delays in getting power to large new housing developments across the UK is a disgrace, but this new proposal to actually generate power on big sites removes the ransom, or strangle hold, you lot have held on progress for quite long enough.'

She signalled to Hogg-Wright, who produced a copy of the fat document in its comb-binder and plastic covers.

'This contains all you need to know about how, from now on, developers will be able to provide essentially free electricity to their buyers, generated on site from gas turbines powered by human waste. It is a clever solution which will unlock countless housing sites across the country.'

Those in the meeting were visibly shocked and looked at each other in bemusement.

'But there is one issue we need to have your agreement on to make this possible, on which the Prime Minister and I expect your full co-operation.' She paused to look at her audience with gimlet eyes. 'Where it will need to be connected to the power networks, hopefully to feed power in, rather than take it out, you will have to approve the system and sanction its connection, and we don't want you sitting on your hands or causing difficulties with this. This is a great opportunity to resolve the housing crisis, generate 'green power' and remove reliance on existing sewage infrastructure from holding up the development of house builder's land banks; and we don't want to do anything to delay it. I trust we understand each other?'

The men and women in the meeting were temporarily struck dumb. They had never been spoken to in such direct terms before by a powerful politician.

At that point Hogg-Wright rose from his seat and opened the door, and in marched a series of assistants, carrying piles of freshly photocopied versions of the document the Home Sec. had in front of her, and began handing them round.

-ooOOoo-

'Sir Jacob Mortimer was here with the Prime Minister, Potty, and they were having a high old time laughing and joking with a gang of the old sweats, as well as some of the newer faces.'

'How interesting, Sebastian,' replied Professor Potts.

'Of course the PM doesn't drink, but the rest were shovelling it away like nobody's business, and they all seemed in a very festive mood.'

'What were they celebrating?'

'Well, I don't know the detail, but Weasel-Face, I mean Hamish Glover, was overheard saying something to the effect that they had put it over the other lot a treat, and wait until the Press got hold of this gem ... Then Sir Jacob Mortimer, who was there with some other financial types, I think, said that they need have no fears about the money being forthcoming to support the house builders, and that was all fixed up.'

'I see,' said the Professor.

'Yes, and I suspect you will like this bit ... The PM then announced that following a series of high-level meetings held today, he expected technical approvals for the system to be used on all these sites, to be forthcoming from all the utility providers shortly. I'm not actually too sure what constitutes a "utility provider", Potty, old man, but I'm assuming it means the faceless gnomes in charge of electricity and drains and so on and so forth.'

'Quite correct, Sebastian.'

'Oh, and there was one other thing ... Weasel-Face said something to the PM to the effect that whoever was behind this deserved a Knighthood. Presumably that means something to you, Potty?'

'Nothing I care to think about too deeply, Sebastian, but thank you once again for a most interesting insight into what goes on in these clubs of yours, and in the corridors of power. Most enlightening.'

-ooOOoo-

Ewan gave each of the row of solid air fresheners positioned on top of the control console a little shake in turn.

'Bloody hell, Dai. If only it would rain!'

'That would certainly help, Ewan. This hot spell is making it nasty. Are you sure all the windows are shut tight?'

'I went round and checked again earlier. I even stuck some sellotape round the edges of one of them because I felt a little draught.'

'That netting they put over it does keep the birds off, I suppose, but it is the flies, man! These ruddy flies!'

'They didn't seem to think about that when they turned on the pumps, did they, Dai. This is getting unbearable.'

'The maintenance blokes think the main silo will be ready to work again next week, but the bits for the turbine still haven't arrived, from somewhere in France, I think it was they said, where they are being made.'

'I heard they were in England but there was some problem at the docks … something to do with Brexit and paperwork holding them up.'

'If it doesn't turn up soon there is going to be a strike by here. The electrical blokes are getting ready to down tools, if you ask me.'

'Oh, don't say that, man! We are on the home straight now, surely!'

-ooo0oo-

TWENTY-SIX

Tim found he was sweating, and it had nothing to do with the warm spell of weather sweeping across the country. The short walk he was about to undertake from his office to Hazel's little bedsit was not what was overheating him either.

What was bothering Tim was that he may be seen carrying an overnight bag by his co-workers; and worse, if any of them knew that a journalist lived where he was going ... such things had led to the downfall of Civil Servants before, and despite the heat, he shuddered. The sooner he was safely inside Hazel's flat and could lose the overnight bag the better.

'Good night, Tim.'

He wheeled round ... it was only Rehema from the Compliance team across the other side of the office.

'Good night, Rehema.' he chanted, just slightly too loud.

Tim avoided the lift and took the almost deserted stairs. There were two cleaners at work but they were both bent over those "Henry" vacuum cleaners with the silly faces, so didn't notice him slip by.

Now on the street, he hastened away from the building.

Not long now, he told himself, and wondered if he should take a less direct route to avoid … To avoid what? Tim shook himself and realised he was being paranoid.

So what if he was going to stay with a friend during a train strike. What business was that of anybody else. It was a free country. Why not?

Having given himself that little talking to, Tim began to feel better.

Not far now.

-oooOoo-

Steve was chopping up chicken for his famous sweet and sour stir-fry when Anne opened the front door and propped her bike in its little hole under the stairs next to his.

'Hi, sweetheart,' he called. 'Hope you are hungry!'

'You betcha!' said Anne grabbing a beer from the fridge and sprawling on the sofa. 'It is hot out there!'

'Did Wally get back OK?'

'Yeah, no problem. He was getting tired though, so I'm glad I went with him to give him a shove up the kerbs and so on.'

'I'm sure he would have managed on his own, you know how independent he is, but I have noticed …'

'Yes, so have I. Do you think we should call his mum?'

'I don't know, Anne. I've been thinking that perhaps we should for a while, but you know how he hates it when she turns up and subjects him to the full mother hen.'

'I hate that for him, too … but we have got to be realistic, Steve. He copes very well on his own, but he would never ask for help so in a way it is for us to keep an eye on him, and look for the signs if he is starting to suffer. He is bound to need support at some stage.'

'It must be awful. Knowing about it, I mean. Knowing that gradually you are going to lose the ability to move, or speak or ...'

'Stop it, Steve, or you will make me cry. I love Wally and I want to help him. I just worry that he might not thank us for unleashing his mother on him again.'

-oo0Ooo-

Surprisingly, Bethany Ford from the National Farmers Union was the hardest to convince of those presented with the fat folder, and was subsequently called in by the Government to discuss it.

The by-product of the bio-digester gas turbine electricity generators is fertiliser which, being created from human excreta, is high in nutrients and performs particularly well when applied to fruit and vegetables. Tomatoes grown in it are especially productive.

After going through the process and then dried, it does not smell either and is free from any harmful 'bugs' which may get into the food chain.

Bethany came from the sort of farming background where, in her experience, the family farm was a nice place to keep her ponies or take the dogs for a walk. She had less of a grasp of the industrialised nature of modern farming and the difficult task of making farming pay.

She found the concept of putting human excrement, however well treated, on the fields difficult, and after her visit to the Welsh facility took some convincing that the 'engineered' enzymes used there could not do the crops any harm, or kill her ponies.

Eventually, surrounded by a collection of some of the greatest scientific brains in the country, headed by Professor Edwin Potts himself, and following lengthy debates with her own scientific advisors, she conceded that perhaps it could work, and agreed on behalf of the wider farming community to back it.

It helped when the calculation of the likely very modest selling price of the fertiliser on the spreadsheets was explained to her, and a handful of her farming advisors said the farmers would be very keen to buy as much of it as they could get their hands on at that price.

It was the last great hurdle, and the selection of six housing development sites, either already in the early stages of being built or about to start, to act as demonstration projects, was swiftly made so that production could commence.

-ooOoo-

TWENTY-SEVEN

'I kept the champagne you sent me, you know, Tim. Shall we open it now?' asked Hazel, swinging her legs out from under the duvet and sitting up.

'Good heavens, it is nearly nine o'clock!' said Tim, catching sight of the alarm clock beside the bed. 'If we are going out for a meal, we had better get on with it, don't you think?'

'Or we could just order in pizza,' said Hazel. 'And besides nine o'clock is almost bedtime for a good little girl like me …'

'Hazel,' smiled Tim. 'Recent events have proved beyond any doubt that you are most certainly not a good little girl. I'm glad to say you are one of the naughtiest girls I think I have ever met …'

'I'm not a good little girl? Oh dear,' She swung her legs back under the quilt again. 'Oh well, the damage is done now. It's too late to do anything about that. Shall I order in pizza to keep your strength up?'

-ooo0oo-

Professor Potts was finding it difficult to settle.

He laid aside his book and tried, yet again, to get the cushions right in his most comfortable chair. But he could not keep intrusive thoughts about how annoyed he had become at Bethany Ford's lumpen inability to understand the facts being presented to her.

He was used to being surrounded by bright young people with open and enquiring minds and constructive ways of debating issues. He knew that years of training had not failed him, and that Ms. Ford would not have discerned his irritation. However, he found her over-privileged monotonous droning about her dogs and ponies eating man-made enzymes a frustrating irrelevance, and found having to repeatedly drag the conversation back to modern farming methods tiresome.

It had emerged in the conversation that Bethany had been friendly with Amanda Trunnion for some years, which might be how she found herself on a 'Government Commission' in the first place, and that Ms. Trunnion's original nominee for the role of Chairman was Giles Norton-Bunkerman, who was Bethany's uncle.

The Professor remembered that the Civil Servant tasked with doing the background checks, before the appointment was made, had to report that the Norton-Bunkerman family had a large shareholding in an American chemical fertiliser company. The Professor wondered briefly if that was why Bethany took so much persuading to accept the fertiliser issue, but he dismissed the idea as implausible, in that it made Bethany appear capable of deeper thought.

Irritating though it had been, he took some comfort from the fact that she was eventually convinced and matters could proceed. But now that it was over he could not settle.

There was a nagging thought in his mind that, in the broad scheme of things, there might be more to the importance of Bethany Ford's family farms to this project than met the eye.

-ooOoo-

Tomorrow, Gordon Sparrow thought, he might well have to face the press for the first time.

He had read the fat document all the way through now, as well as the in-depth report of what happened in Wales in The Gazette, and had more of a grasp of what it was all about, but he still felt very unprepared.

Glancing at his wristwatch, he noticed that it was a little after nine o'clock and the debate in the Commons Chamber was droning on. There were only a handful of MP's present and he wondered if he could slip away and return later for the vote.

He felt very tired and thought perhaps nobody would notice if he popped up to his little office, closed the door and got forty winks.

He was on his way through the corridor at the back of the Commons Chamber when he encountered Hamish Glover coming the other way.

'Sparrow, isn't it? Gordon Sparrow. Ah yes. Glad I bumped into you as I wanted a word.'

Gordon was quite alarmed at the unexpected approach. In the past Cabinet Ministers had swept past him and seemed oblivious to his very existence when they passed in corridors.

'How are you settling in, old chap? Got your office sorted out? Right, right.'

Gordon nodded, smiled and made what he hoped were appropriate noises.

'Look, firstly, before I forget, I wanted a word about your Civil Servant chappy, Patrick Blenny. How do you find him? Bit of an old woman, by all accounts. Anyway, the thing is that he put in for a transfer when Amanda Trunnion had your job and it has just come through. He is going to Housing.'

'Oh,' said Gordon. 'I see.'

'I've been hearing very good reports about his deputy, Jim; no not Jim …'

'Tim,' offered Gordon.

'Yes … Tim. That's it. Tim Blande. It's your department of course, so your decision, but you might like to ask him to take over from Blenny. I've heard he handled the press very competently in Wales when the bio-digester plant blew up. Having someone who is capable and experienced when dealing with them by your side might be a help, at least until you are more settled in.'

A great sense of relief washed over Gordon.

'He seems very pleasant,' he managed to say.

'Good, good. Right, well the real reason I wanted to speak to you was to invite you to lunch at Osbert's Club one day next week. I think you will find it useful and interesting and there are several people there I would like you to meet. My PPS will call you tomorrow to fix it up. Oh! There is the division bell … back to work!'

Gordon had never heard of Osbert's Club, but he was relieved to discover that Tim … Tim Blande, that was it; that Tim was confident in dealing with the press. He had been very nervous about encountering them, and now he could have someone alongside him who not only was used to it, but who was also approved by a senior Cabinet Minister.

Gordon's tiredness had evaporated, and as he walked back into the Chamber alongside Hamish Glover, no less, he felt on top of the world.

-oooOoo-

'Wow!' said Anne Pickles. 'This email says they want a meeting prior to placing an order for six complete systems in various locations to act as demonstration projects!'

'Yes! We have done it!' Steve was already sending a WhatsApp message to Wally and an email to Professor Potts to tell them the good news.

'Yes, but now the real work starts,' said Anne. 'We will have to set up teams to do the monitoring once they are installed and to watch over how they are constructed too.'

'Best start putting the word out in our little network then.'

'Oh, Steve,' said Anne, snuggling up close to him on the sofa. 'Isn't this exciting!'

TWENTY-EIGHT

'Hazel! I just got promoted!' said Tim excitedly into his mobile phone as the door of the Gents toilet closed behind him.

The interview, first thing this morning, had been brief, and that awful smart-arse Darren Southwood from HR presided over it as if the whole thing was his idea. But there was no denying the outcome.

Following his successful request for a transfer, Patrick Blenny was moving to Housing, and the Minister himself had asked if Tim could be offered the job as his replacement!

Although he looked as though he was sucking a lemon as he passed the news along, there was no denying that Darren had to do as he was told, and Tim's appointment would be confirmed with immediate effect. It moved him up one pay Grade as well, so represented a slight salary increase. But the best part was that he would have his own office, rather than just a space in the open-plan area.

It was so unexpected that Tim could not keep still as he told Hazel the news, and rather imprudently he had not checked to see if there was anyone else in the toilets when he made his call.

Blenkinsop from Compliance flushed, came out of a cubical and moved past Tim to wash his hands.

'Congratulations, Tim. Well deserved,' he said.

-ooOoo-

Henry McCray, the Production Manager at Ceylex Engineering, who oversaw the manufacture of the first pressurised mini-silo and the gas turbine unit, confirmed that he would be delighted to meet Anne and Steve and 'their team' to discuss producing six more complete units.

He could arrange a meeting, alongside Balance Electrical Systems, who were also involved in the first one, as soon as they liked, he said.

'Good,' said Anne. 'But we will need a meeting room on the ground floor preferably, and with wheelchair access as our, erm, Chief Engineer has some mobility issues.'

'Oh,' said Henry McCray. 'Leave it with me and I'm sure we can sort something out.'

-ooOoo-

'It was the best laugh I've had all year, Potty, old man!' Sebastian Burleigh-Marks chortled as he prepared to tell the Professor the events he had witnessed.

'Weasel-Face, I mean Hamish Glover, had arranged to meet this funny little Sparrow chap for lunch, and the poor blighter was obviously so far out of his comfort zone that it was painful to watch.'

'Oh dear. Are we talking about Gordon Sparrow, Amanda Trunnion's replacement?'

'Got it in one, Potty. Got it in one.'

'I see.'

'Well, when the little Sparrow turned up, Weasel-Face and Horrid, I mean Horace Smithson, had been sucking down champagne-cocktails with the old brigade for some time, so a mellow glow pervaded the pre-lunch bar gathering. Weasel-Face introduced Sparrow all round and the poor blighter almost had his hand shaken off. Then the tape went up and they were off to the dining room.'

'Go on.'

'Well, I was fortunate to be dining with Grumpy Burton and a couple of the chaps from the Carlton Club, over for a visit. With a bit of my customary skullduggery, I squeezed my chair round so that I had my back to old Horrid, and while I couldn't see the merry throng, I could hear every word.'

'And what were they discussing, Sebastian?'

'Hang on, a bit more scenario painting is called for first,' chuckled Sebastian. 'When Horrid tottered off to the loo, Weasel-Face turned to the Sparrow and said, in so many words, not to get too close to Horrid because he would sell his grandmother for the chance to get back closer to the driving seat, and when sober at least, was quite likely to tell the press any old story to further his agenda.'

'Yes, I think we have seen the former Prime Minister doing that sort of thing before ...'

'Indeed we have, so no news there. But when he came back from the toilet, Weasel-Face had to leave the table to take a phone call, and that is when Horrid clasped the Sparrow's arm and told him not to get too tied up with Weasel-Face because he would stab anyone in the back and twist the knife if it suited his aims and objects, without a thought for old friendships and loyalty.'

'There is no love lost between those two then ...'

'Oh no, Potty. Most of the time they are a thick as thieves and go about like a couple of old comrades. It is only in matters of power that they get a bit prickly.'

'Really. How interesting.'

'Well, anyway. Against that background the Sparrow then had to eat his lunch, and the poor little runt was on the back foot when the menu was presented. It was in French as it happens. You could see he didn't have much of a clue what he was looking at when, following Weasel-Face's lead, he ordered the steak-tartare, and then the silly poop sent it back because it was cold!'

'Oh dear me.'

'I could see the waiters were still tittering about that one when Horrid, who was well oiled by this time, decided to have some fun. He called for the dessert wine menu and said "perhaps you would like to choose for us Mr. Sparrow." Well, inevitably the poor little chap hadn't a clue what to do, but Weasel-Face, annoyed by this behaviour, came to his rescue and announced his own favourite tipple from the list, which of course was what the Sparrow then ordered. He went on to tell Horrid to lay off the poor little chap in none too quiet a tone.'

'How unfortunate. Is dining at this club of yours always like this?'

'Oh no. Sometimes it is much worse. Anyway, Potty, old man, the thing that would interest you, I'm sure, occurred when they left the dining table and went for coffee in the lounge. By that time Horrid was pretty much out of it so a couple of his chums organised to get him off home and most of his entourage went with him. That just left Weasel-Face and Sir Jacob Mortimer, and then they were joined by a chap called Jeff Bishop, who I happen to know is the Chief Executive of Diospyros Developments, the biggest property developer in the country. They are the group that own Pomegranate Homes as well as all sorts of other national and regional house builders you have probably heard of.'

'Yes, I've heard of them,' said the Professor.

'Anyway, old Grumpy and I had said goodbye to our chums by then and we were free to take up a strategic position in the coffee lounge area, close enough to Weasel-Face's part of the room to hear most, if not all, of what was being said.'

'How convenient.'

'Yes. This Jeff Bishop chappy was flapping round Sir Jacob Mortimer and being introduced to the Sparrow and was ordering brandies all round and what not, when Weasel-Face asked him if he had placed the order for the first six demonstration projects. I assume that means something to you, Potty?'

'It does.'

'Well, Jeff Bishop hedged a bit at that, and was saying something about needing to approve the company supplying them and doing financial background checks and what not, when much to my surprise, Weasel-Face went red in the face, thumped the coffee table and said "we don't have time for all that sort of nonsense". That made the Sparrow jump as you might expect, at which point Sir Jacob Mortimer raised his hand and said "Jeff, you need have no concerns about fast-tracking this," and everyone looked at him in astonishment.'

'How alarming. Then what happened?'

'Well, then old Mortimer said that the company supplying the units had a line of credit through his own organisation which would more than guarantee their financial stability for the purposes of this project.'

'I see.'

'Well, then I got drawn off into a rather diverting little game of cards with Grumpy and some other fellows and lost the thread for a while. But I caught up after that Jeff Bishop cove had left, and as Sir Jacob was saying his farewells. At that point I heard Weasel-Face asking him if it was true that this company they had been discussing was being funded by Sir Jacob's outfit … and he came over all smiles and said "Of course not, Hamish. I've never heard of them. But we don't want a little detail like that holding the project up, do we?" And guess what … old Weasel-face got to his feet, shook his hand and said "Thank you very much, Jacob. That was very kind of you." I've no idea what the little Sparrow thought of all that because he was sitting with his back to me, but I suspect his initiation into the wheels within wheels of these matters has been an interesting one.'

'Sebastian, once again you surpass my hopes and expectations for our little arrangement. Well done indeed!'

When Professor Potts had said goodbye to Sebastian, he dialled Sir Jacob Mortimer's number and left a message for him to call back about a small company looking for funding for a project involving a Government contract, who he would like to introduce him to.

-ooo0oo-

TWENTY-NINE

'So he asked me if it would be sensible to meet representatives of The Gazette to discuss the Wales situation, and cited your article about it as being useful, Hazel.'

'I'm flattered. What did you say Tim?'

'I said that meeting you made sense, and that if he wanted I could attend as well. He liked that idea and asked me to call you, so that is why I'm calling now.'

'Oh, not to tell me that I am adorable and beg me for another date then?'

'Well, no. I mean yes. You are of course, and I do, want another date, I mean. But I have to call you on business …'

'And you can rest assured that I want another date too, Tim. But in the meantime, when do I get to meet the fascinating Mr. Sparrow?'

-ooOoo-

The two big blue fly-zappers now installed in the control room certainly helped a bit, but every time the door opened a new cloud of flies burst in.

'Bit of news, I've got, Ewan, man,' said Dai.

'Oh yes?'

'Yes. It seems the Home Secretary herself has intervened after our Minister complained about the delay, and the turbine parts have been released from the docks, and are on their way here as we speak.'

'Well, thank goodness for that, and about time too! What was holding them up?'

'Brexit,' said Dai, and with no further explanation needed, Ewan returned to his crossword.

-ooo0oo-

'So if you are happy with that, Anne,' said Professor Potts, 'the date is in the diary.'

'Thanks, Professor. Now, can we set a little time aside to go over what we are, and more importantly are not, supposed to say to these financial people, please?'

'Certainly, although, as you know I am not very experienced in the world of finance, so my advice may not be of much use …'

'But if Professor Misato Ho, the incoming head of the Physics Faculty is, as you say, over from America and will be able to come to the meeting, with you there too, we have some big hitters from the science side of things.'

'You are very kind, Anne, although I fear my own contribution will be fairly insignificant. It is however, a happy coincidence that Misato is going to be here. Will Wally Walters be able to join us?'

'Yes, of course, he will be there.'

'Anne, I've been meaning to ask why Wally is not one of the

directors of your Company, erm ... Bio-Power Solutions (Oxford) Ltd. isn't it?' said the Professor. 'He did pretty much single handedly develop the mini bio-digester and turbine, after all.'

'Ah, that is a ticklish subject, Professor. You know that Wally has motor-neurone disease, and he knows ...' Anne could not keep the catch out of her voice. 'He knows the prognosis. So, he feels that he would rather just have shares in the company so that, if it does well, he gets some of the profit to make his life a bit more comfortable, but does not have to bother with the spadework. He keeps saying he could be a drag on the business side of things and wouldn't have anything to contribute anyway. He wants to be free to spend his time working on this mobility scooter shop rider thing, powered by bottled bio-digester generated gas he has been working on, as well. He says he has got it working well and now needs to concentrate on creating a way to stop it smelling so foul, so he can think about finding a market for it.'

'Ah, poor Wally. Pragmatic he may be, but it is a shame he feels he cannot participate fully.'

'Well, if we do well, he does well, Professor. When Steve and I set Bio-Power Solutions up, we allocated just three shares, so the ownership of the company is split three ways between Wally, Steve and I. Naturally we have underwritten Wally's liability personally, so if we fail or lose money, he will never have any debt or liability to the business.'

'I knew you would have that side of things in hand, Anne. I look forward to seeing you all at the meeting then!'

'Yes. But, before you go are you sure I can't convince you to take some of the profits yourself if we succeed, Professor?'

'No Anne, we have been through all this. My role is to mentor. Nothing else. My reward will be to see you, and all our young friends succeeding.'

'Is there nothing we can do to ...'

'Well, occasional help in the garden would be handy. Did I say thank you properly for pruning the apple trees the other week?'

-ooOOoo-

'Next item on the agenda,' Gordon Sparrow told himself, 'find out how to read French menus. Don't want a repeat of that steak tartare incident.'

He was on his way to a meeting with Hazel and Tim during which he would undertake his first press interview. He wasn't looking forward to it, but at least if Tim was going to be there, he would have some support.

'Pretty impressive chap, this Tim, when you get to know him a bit,' thought Gordon. 'Certainly knows his way around the press issue. I wonder if he knows how to read a French menu?'

-ooOOoo-

'No, not Twig; it is Trigg with an 'r' and two 'g's', but please call me Hazel,' said Hazel.

'I do beg your pardon,' said Gordon.

'Don't worry about it, Minister, it has been happening all my life. At school it was usually "Twiglet" rather than just mis-spelling Trigg.'

'Ha, I can sympathise with that … they used to call me "Bird-Brain" at school … Sparrow, you see …'

'I think the Minister would prefer it if you didn't mention that, Hazel,' said Tim.

'Oh gosh …' said Gordon, blushing deeply.

'Don't worry, I have forgotten it already,' smiled Hazel.

'Th .. th .. thank you,' stammered Gordon.

'So, Minister, I see you went to the same school as the Prime Minister. Did you see much of each other there?'

Gordon pulled himself together and took a deep breath.

'No, not much, actually. The PM was two years ahead of me, you see, and there wasn't really any opportunity.'

'But you knew he was at the school?'

'Oh yes. I saw him about.'

'Was he very sporty? I see you learned to sail there, was that something the Prime Minister did too?'

'Er, not as far as I was aware. He might have done, I suppose, but not with me.'

'You are quite a proficient solo sailor, aren't you, Minister?'

'Please call me Gordon, Hazel. I'm not used to all this "Minister" stuff quite yet.'

'Thank you, Gordon, it makes a good deal of difference to our readers if we can humanise our politicians by using first names. Going back to sailing then, Gordon, didn't you once make "Morning Mist" your boat, your home for three months? Was that a planned trip.'

'I ... I ... er. Well, you see I was very much younger then and ... and ...'

'This was before you had any ties of employment wasn't it, Minister,' said Tim helpfully.

'Er, yes. Yes. That was it ...' said Gordon catching on to Tim's lead. 'In days gone by, young men such as myself might have taken themselves off on what was called "the grand tour", but such extravagance was beyond my means, so three months pottering about on my boat had to suffice.'

'I see. And where did you go during this extended youthful excursion?'

'Oh, you know. Here and there … I spent a while exploring the French coast …'

'Visiting the casinos?'

'Casinos? No, nothing like that. I don't gamble and even if I did, I didn't have the wherewithal back then.'

'Did your family know where you were?'

'I … I … We … erm …'

'Perhaps you would like to discuss the Commission and the Minister's work with the team that is to decontaminate the site in Wales now, Hazel. I'm afraid there are many calls upon the Minister's time, and we can't spare him too much longer,' said Tim.

'Ah, yes,' said Gordon. 'That is all coming together very well, perhaps I could explain about the programme the Commission is overseeing, in conjunction with the Welsh authorities, and which we developed with our partners …'

Gordon began to relax and soon got into his stride now that the subject matter was impersonal and he felt on safer ground.

-ooo0oo-

THIRTY

'So you don't blame me, then?'

'No, I suppose not, Hazel. That is your job after all.'

'I bet there *is* something juicy in this three-month trip on his boat to come out though, Tim. Just a pity that, with you to manage him, he is not going to let it slip to me.'

'I do quite value my job, you know Hazel, and anything for a quiet life!'

'I quite value you, you know, Tim,' said Hazel, kissing him on the forehead. 'And I'm only sorry that you have to go home this evening so I can't wrap you up in my wicked spider's web again.'

'I shouldn't really have come back here after work anyway, Hazel. The trains are still all over the place, and I don't know what time I shall be able to get home as it is.'

'Aren't you glad you came back here first, then?'

'Yes, although I don't seem to have had that cup of tea you talked about before we …'

'Tea, be blowed. The next train is at 7:45,' said Hazel, having checked the app on her mobile phone again, as she stretched out seductively on the sofa bed. 'Just enough time, I think.'

'Hazel, you are insatiable,' said Tim, wrapping her in his arms.

'I'm afraid so. But you don't seem to mind, so lucky me!'

-oooOoo-

As a direct appointment, made personally by Amanda Trunnion, when Piers Aubin heard that his services were no longer required by the Government Commission, he was not surprised.

He had plenty of work anyway, and even if it was only for a brief spell, being invited to join a Government Commission did look good on his c.v., and he would milk it for all it was worth when encouraging new clients to put their public profiles in his hands.

The fact that Amanda had been sacked and his ideas for selling the story had not exactly been crowned with glory would soon be forgotten, even if anyone actually noticed. The plain fact that he had been invited to join a Government Commission did wonders for his profile, and he was happy enough to leave it at that.

-oooOoo-

Sitting in the coffee shop afterwards, Professor Edwin Potts, Professor Misato Ho, Anne Pickles, Wally Walters and Steve Browning all agreed that the meeting had gone well.

Quite exceptionally well, it seemed. The financiers present had asked for a 'walk through' of the figures Anne provided, and asked Wally and the two Professors to describe how the system worked, and that was it, really.

'They've been put under pressure to approve this,' said Misato. 'I think the Government don't have any more options, so this is the best they can do.'

'Now that the concept of the bio-digester and turbine has gained public recognition, it could be that the politicians feel obligated to deliver something positive,' said Steve.

'I know little of the inner workings of financiers' minds,' said Professor Potts. 'But it would make sense for them to want to be involved in something which is, after all, underwritten by some of the largest and most successful property developers in the country, especially as the Government has so publicly supported it.'

'So tomorrow we have our meeting with Ceylex Engineering and Balance Electrical Systems, and we can be much more confident in that meeting after today,' said Anne.

'And on Monday, the all-important meeting with the bosses and advisors of Diospyros Developments. That is the big one,' said Wally.

-ooOOoo-

Ewan gave Dai a 'high five' as, from the relative comfort of the control centre, they watched the three large lorries leave the site having unloaded the long-awaited turbine parts at last.

'Now we will see some progress,' he said.

'We nearly lost the electrical people last week, mind. If we hadn't got it agreed and ordered in that team to spray insecticide about and kill some of the flies off, they would have downed tools, I'm sure.'

'It was a bit better after they got those water sprinklers set up by here. I agree that spraying that stuff has made a lot of difference, even if we do have to wear breathing apparatus when we go outside, at least for a while until it completely clears.'

'The bloke who drove that big spray tanker said the stuff they use has been made illegal in the EU now, but since Brexit he can still use it here. We do have to be careful not to breathe it in, mind. Kills anything, that does, he said.'

'Let's hope it doesn't kill off the maintenance teams before they get the ruddy turbine rebuilt and us up and running, ay?'

'I think it's more likely that the smell, when they start pumping the contents of what was the caravan site back out, will be what kills them. I'm thinking of taking annual leave when they do that!'

'I've been meaning to talk to you about annual leave, actually. I think it would be best if we both put in for a couple of weeks when the plant is re-commissioned and running again. Then they can bring in temporary staff to keep an eye on it while we clear off and get some sun …'

-oooOoo-

Philip Knowles called his senior assistants into his office in the headquarters of the Environment Agency.

'I've just had an email from Sir Barton Parish, the head of the Highways Agency,' he announced. 'He is saying that … hang-on, probably easier if I read this out … Ah, yes … "after considerable work" … blah, blah, blah, "can now confirm that the previous objections" … and so on and so forth … "although we still have reservations about one or two of the schemes, the main bulk of them now have solutions which can be implemented from a Highways perspective, if the Environment Agency can confirm their support." What all that means is old Sir Barton has got his finger out and found ways to solve the problems on the list of sites awaiting Planning decisions, and is now passing it off to us to give the OK from the Environment Agency's viewpoint.'

He looked around the room and drew in a deep breath.

'Right. Now the onus is on us to clear our objections and remove any hurdles, or create acceptable mitigations, and get these schemes up and running. The Government want spades in the ground yesterday, if not before. Any questions?'

-oooOoo-

'What's next?' thought Gordon Sparrow as he sat at his little desk in Portcullis House, adjacent to the houses of Parliament.

There were several debates he wanted to attend later on, in the Commons Chamber, and he needed to do some preparation for his first Constituency Surgery since becoming a Minister, due in a couple of weeks' time. He wondered if Tim could be present at that.

Did a Minister's Civil Servants work on a Saturday? He would have to ask. If Tim could come, would he mind the long trip up to coastal Norfolk at the weekend? The MP's surgery in Gordon's constituency had always been held on a Saturday, but that didn't mean it had to be. Many MP's held theirs on a Friday. He would ask Tim if he could move it to a Friday, and if so could Tim come along.

As he dialled Tim's number, he glanced up at the picture of his yacht "Morning Mist" on the wall and shook his head. 'Not this weekend, I'm afraid, my lovely,' he muttered.

-oo0Ooo-

THIRTY-ONE

Ceylex Engineering didn't have a ground floor meeting room that Wally could comfortably use, so they had booked a 'conference room' in a nearby hotel for the meeting.

Their colleagues from Balance Electrical Systems had got there early and everything was ready for the meeting when Anne, Steve and Wally arrived.

Rather than turn up in the old bread van, Steve had borrowed his mother's BMW, which although not new by any stretch of the imagination, did look a little more appropriate for a business meeting of this type, especially after he had given it a wash.

Henry McCray, the Production Manager from Ceylex Engineering, met them at the hotel reception desk and showed them through to the meeting room, where they were introduced to Des Montague, Ceylex Managing Director, and Sam Warburton, Business Development Manager, from Balance Electrical Systems.

After the coffee, tea and biscuits had been distributed, they got down to business.

-ooo0oo-

'So Weasel-Face, I mean Hamish Glover, was in high spirits and was telling everyone who would listen that this deal he had masterminded would solve so many problems that, in and of itself, it ought to guarantee the Conservatives blowing away the other lot and gaining an increased majority at the next General Election.'

'Very bold, and potentially a little premature, Sebastian,' said Professor Potts.

'Well, perhaps,' said Sebastian. 'But you can't blame him for wanting to celebrate his success, Potty.'

'Of course not. I am delighted to hear that they view it all so positively.'

'Yes. That Jeff Bishop, the property developer chap, turned up next with a couple of other fellows I didn't recognise and the mood got very festive. I overheard a bit of conversation about the Highways people being satisfied and confirmation of … hold on, now, what did he say? Oh yes … confirmation that connection to the National Grid would be available for all but three of the sites; I think he said. Does that ring any bells, Potty?'

'It does Sebastian, and is very good news.'

'We aim to please …'

'And as usual, you have done, Sebastian. Thank you very much indeed.'

-oo0Ooo-

'So long as we don't have to go for a watercress tea, Tim.'

'Not if you don't want to Hazel. But we did have a plan to go and spend some time in the country, and we haven't done it yet.'

'Actually, I've had a much better idea that will not involve getting a car and would be rather fun. The week after next, how about we go to Brighton for the weekend. We could do it by train and stay in a hotel by the sea.'

'Brighton?'

'What's wrong with Brighton? The ideal place for a weekend escape, I would have thought.'

'Well, yes. Very nice.'

'You are thinking of it as a dirty weekend in Brighton, aren't you, Tim!'

'No, Hazel, not at all. It was just a bit of surprise …'

'I'd love it if you took me away for a weekend in Brighton, Tim. We could walk along the beach hand in hand, play crazy golf by the pier, and I'll even buy you an ice cream if you are good.'

'OK. Why not! Shall I find a suitable hotel?'

'Well, most of the cheap ones used for dirty weekends are a couple of rows back from the sea where the views from the windows don't matter so much. But I've always wanted to stay in the Grand Hotel; you know the one where Maggie Thatcher and her entourage got blown up in 1984. It sounds elegant and lovely, and has wonderful sea views.'

'Oh. Erm … Do you know how much it might cost?'

'I'll go halves with you Tim, if you like.'

'So you *do* know how much then, Hazel …'

'Well, I did check it out, yes.'

'And?'

'Well, the sea view rooms are more expensive, of course, but what would be the point if you didn't have one of those. No sea view and it *would* be like a dirty weekend. And we don't have to eat there if the menu prices are a bit rich ....'

'How much, Hazel?'

'About £250 a night.'

'How much!'

'Each. A sea view room is around £500 a night ...'

There was silence on the other end of the phone line.

'Tim?'

'Well, you did warn me that you had Rolls Royce tastes, I suppose.'

'And it would be rather special. A memory we could treasure for ever.'

'That is a lot of money for a hotel room ...'

'OK, make it two ice creams and I'll pay for the crazy golf.'

'Do you always get your way, Hazel?'

'I'm not sure ... do I, Tim?'

'Half each, you say?'

'All right you are on, but I'm paying for one of those ice creams you mentioned.'

'Really?'

'Yes. All right. Go on then, let's spoil ourselves.'

'Oh Tim! Thank you! I've been wanting to stay at the Grand Hotel ever since we used to go to Brighton on holiday when I was a little girl and we walked past it on our way back to our caravan!'

'Very well. Leave it to me and I'll get it booked.'

-ooOoo-

'Well, I zoned out for a bit when you started talking about an improvement to the, now what was it ... the high-pressure anti back-wash collar ...'

'The back-pressure upper collet flange, I think that was, Anne,' laughed Wally.

'Yes, well. Whatever. But apart from all that technical geekery and gobbledygook, I thought the meeting went very well,' said Anne.

'So did I,' said Steve as he turned out of the hotel car park onto the main road. 'The figures they were coming up with were all pretty much what we had expected ...'

'And the delivery timescales were better than I thought they would be,' added Wally.

'Yes. And the factory has more capacity than we originally thought, so we might be able to put more units through there before we need to involve other manufacturers.' Anne concluded.

'So, we might actually be able to pull this off,' said Wally. 'If we don't get too badly skinned alive by the property developers on Monday, we are rolling.'

'Do you think they will try to skin us?' Steve asked.

'They are property developers, sweetheart. It comes with the territory,' said Anne. 'Although we must not lose sight of the fact that they currently have no other choice but to deal with us, and without us they don't get their planning permissions.'

'The Professor has got something up his sleeve about that, I'm sure,' Wally said.

'Any idea what?'

'Not a clue, but I bet it will be good.'

-ooOoo-

THIRTY-TWO

'So, if I have understood you correctly, the good news,' said Sir Jacob Mortimer, 'is that all but one of the demonstration sites is ready to proceed, although three on the longer list of all the sites you put forward nationwide still can't go ahead?'

'That's right,' said Jeff Bishop, taking a long draught of his beer. 'I call that a pretty good result given the difficulties we have encountered with these sites over the last five or ten years.'

'And you have got the local MP to get the Minister responsible to visit the demonstration site which still has a problem to try and resolve the issues?'

'Yes, in a couple of weeks' time. That site is in Norfolk, just outside Norwich, but in the Constituency next door to the responsible Minister. He is that Gordon Sparrow chap we met at your club who is heading this up now. He will meet the local MP and some of the interested parties on site then.'

'What is the problem with this site, Jeff?'

'It is part of a long term twenty-thousand-unit scheme in the area covered by Broadwater District Council, just outside Norwich, and was going to be one of the last phases to be built out because it needs a big electricity step-down transformer and substation to be built and running first. That is not programmed to be started for five years. It also has planning permission for 125 houses but only has a drainage discharge capacity for 60 units at present, so it was pushed way back in the programme until all the infrastructure improvements catch up. If we can get the Minister to unravel the electricity problems we can speed up the drainage improvements planned, then we can build out all 125 units, against which we can also fund the works to a substantial area of POS adjacent.'

'POS?'

'Sorry, Public Open Space. It is where we have to provide a swing park and football fields and so on eventually, but it is right next to the site in question and would be the ideal place to put the bio-digester and turbine, partly underground. We could even give the Council a dry ski slope if they like, by tucking the bio-digester silo under the high bit of the ski slope to hide it and avoid the costs of having to dig it into the ground too much,' chuckled Jeff.

'Well, that all sounds splendid, Jeff. Let me see what pressure I can bring to bear from this end. If Hamish Glover can be encouraged to push the transformer and sub-station thing along, and you can speed up the drainage infrastructure, given that it is part of a new substantial development already on site, it should get the project up and running quickly. That will do wonders for the public perception of all this.'

'That is just what I thought, Sir Jacob,' said Jeff.

'Would you care for another beer?' said Sir Jacob as he sought to catch the landlord's eye from the pub garden where they sat.

-oo0Ooo-

'It is scheduled for the weekend after next, on the Saturday,' said Gordon Sparrow. 'I tried to move it to the Friday. I can move these meetings to Fridays in the future, but this time my Constituency Office want me to go for a meeting afterwards with some protestors on a site just outside Norwich. It is one of the six demonstration sites for the bio-digester turbine plants you see, and although it is actually in the neighbouring constituency to mine, the local Broadwater MP wants to meet me there ...'

'And you want me to accompany you?'

'Well, I know it is an imposition at the weekend and so on and so forth, but this is rather important, and I would be very grateful if you could.'

'To both meetings?'

'Yes, if you wouldn't mind. The Constituency Surgery is planned to take place in a little hall in the town of Cromer, by the sea. Obviously, there will be a hotel stay involved for you, so if you could see your way clear to coming, why not bring your family and give them a weekend on the beach?'

'Well, I suppose, if you wish it, Minister ...'

'Great! Thank you, Tim, this means a lot to me. I shall be going up on the train on Friday night quite late, but so long as you can be there for the surgery at eleven o'clock on the Saturday morning, feel free to make your own arrangements to get there.'

Having finished the call, Tim sighed. Now he had to decide whether to call the Grand Hotel in Brighton first to cancel their booking, or if he should start by telling Hazel their plans had just been disrupted.

-oo0Ooo-

In Professor Potts' garden, Anne spread out the table cloth and arranged the chairs around the old wooden table by the French doors.

As Wally organised the cups and saucers, and Steve returned from a walk around the garden to admire the roses, the Professor went to open the front door to Professor Misato Ho, who had just arrived by taxi.

'Well, thank you all for coming,' the Professor said, as he emerged from the kitchen a few moments later carrying a heavily-laden tray. 'I baked a cake. I hope it will be all right.'

The cake, on an old-fashioned glass pedestal stand looked magnificent, and the scones, jam and cream the Professor also unloaded from the tray, soon had everyone crowding round the table licking their lips.

'That looking good, Edwin!' said Misato. 'Did you bake the scones too?'

'The scones are my grandmother's recipe,' said Professor Potts. 'Largely infallible even for a cook as bad as me. Do tuck in.'

'Somebody have to help me here,' said Misato, picking up a warm scone. 'Is it jam then cream or the other way round? In Japan there are similar eating conventions and the host can be offended if you caught doing it the wrong way!'

Everyone laughed at that, and they all enjoyed the excellent tea.

Bees buzzed about their business, birds sang in the apple trees and the wonderful summer colours of the flowers in the Professor's prolific flowerbeds looked at their absolute best in the sunny garden, which all made for a pleasant and relaxed afternoon.

'Erm ...' said the Professor at length, breaking the silence as his guests enjoyed their cake. 'I think I ought to tell you about the next stage of the plan.'

'Right-ho, Professor,' said Wally, as Anne helped him to a second slice of cake. 'I've been wondering what you had up your sleeve.'

'Very perceptive, young Wally,' smiled the Professor. 'I hope you are going to like it and won't think it is too much.'

'Come on Professor,' said Steve. 'Spill the beans.'

'Very well. Could I have another cup of tea, please Anne, while you are pouring.'

'Here you are, Professor, now what's this all about?' said Anne.

'Well, you see, it has come to my notice that the Saturday after next, Gordon Sparrow, the MP who now leads the Commission for the Government, has a meeting on a building site which was on the original list to be one of the much-publicised demonstration projects. This site is the one up in Norfolk where there are some problems which might mean it cannot be used for our project.'

'Go on,' said Wally.

'I happen to know that there are going to be some members of the public at this meeting ... Are the protesters ready, Misato?'

'You just have to say the word and they will assemble as agreed,' nodded Misato.

'Right. Well, there are going to be the usual collection of objectors to any development taking place on the site when the MP's and some press people get there, but some other demonstrators with a rather different agenda will also be there.'

'What on earth are you up to, Professor?' said Anne.

'Well you see, our protestors, if I may call them that, will be handing out leaflets and holding placards, if I am not mistaken, Misato ...'

'Quite correct, Edwin.'

'Holding placards demanding that they too should have free 'green' electricity and promoting the message that our bio-digester powered turbines should be rolled out across the country and the benefits made available to all, not just a few privileged new house buyers. It should cause quite an amusing diversion, and it will be interesting to see what the press make of it.'

'Professor, that is brilliant!' said Steve. 'Just as the initial Press and media interest might be beginning to die down on this story, you pep it right up again with highly visible public support for the idea.'

'Well, it was just a thought,' smiled the Professor.

'Who are these demonstrators?' asked Anne.

'You probably know most of them,' said Misato. 'They all former students of ours or their families and friends.'

'Blimey!' said Wally.

-ooOOoo-

THIRTY-THREE

'And, I'm sorry, as I said, Hazel. Although I know it won't be as good, there are two similarities at least.'

'Which are?'

'Erm …' Tim shuffled his feet. 'Both the hotels have sea views, and as it happens, they are both called The Grand Hotel.'

'But one is in Cromer where you have to go for work, while I suppose you expect me to sit about knitting or something, awaiting the return of my Lord and Master!'

'Well, actually it might get rather more interesting than that for you, from a professional point of view.'

'You are making it up! The last interesting thing that happened in Cromer was probably a visit by Queen Victoria.'

'Well, I don't know about that. But there is going to be a demonstration on the building site the Minister is visiting after his constituency meeting, so that might be something you can cover for The Gazette perhaps …'

'Herrumph!'

'Well at least we will be together, and I could buy you a Cromer crab supper …'

'Ah, well as it happens, I like crab, so that is a possibility. I suppose it was much less pricey too …'

'Yes. The price of the hotel room for both of us is going to be £209 including breakfast, and because I realise it is a disappointment, I will cover the cost. We can use a car from the car club to get there too.'

'That's all right, Tim. We said we would split it and we still can. But you can pay for the Cromer crab tea, as your punishment for spoiling my trip to Brighton.'

-ooOOoo-

By the time Jeff Bishop joined the meeting, in the plush boardroom at the offices of Diospyros Developments, Anne, Wally and Steve had already been grilled by various staff members and technical advisers about how the bio-digester and turbine system was to be manufactured, to confirm that they had the financial wherewithal to complete the project, and asked for guarantees in relation to delivery timings.

When Jeff Bishop came in, Wally turned his chair slightly to enable him to comfortably shake hands, but in so doing he upset his cup of tea, which spilled over the meeting table.

'Does he want a fresh cup?' Jeff asked, ignoring the hand which Wally held out to shake as Anne hastily mopped up the mess.

'Why don't you ask him?' said Anne, looking furious. 'He can understand perfectly well and speak for himself, you know.'

'I'm sorry,' said Jeff, flustered. 'I just thought, you know, with the wheelchair …'

'Anne, it's fine …' Wally started to say.

'You didn't think at all!' said Anne, rising from her chair. 'You just made an assumption that Wally was disabled, so was somehow of lesser value than the rest of us!'

'Leave it, Anne,' pleaded Steve. But Anne was on her feet now with her hands on her hips.

'This man, Mr. Bishop,' said Anne, placing one hand on Wally's shoulder, 'is the reason we are all here today and because of his genius you might get planning permission to build out your sites and make a fortune. Wally here invented this system and built the first one himself with his own hands. So show him some respect!' And with that she sat down.

'I'm sorry, Mr. Bishop... Anne doesn't mean ...' Wally started to say.

'Perhaps we could ...' Steve began to say.

'No, I'm the one who should apologise,' said Jeff. 'I spoke without thinking and allowed the awful outdated attitudes I was bought up with to come to the surface. Wally, what I said was unforgivable.'

'Please, there is no need, Mr. Bishop. It's fine. As you might imagine that is not the first time things like that have happened to me, and nor will it be the last,' said Wally. 'Thank you, Anne, for leaping to my defence, but we just need to calm down now and get on with the job in hand, I think.'

'That is very magnanimous of you Wally,' said the head of the largest property development company in the country. 'I may swank about in smart boardrooms now, but I left school and started work on a building site when I was fifteen, and I'm afraid I picked up the attitudes of those around me in a tough environment. I sometimes slip up badly, as I did just now, and I still have much to learn about life. I am truly sorry.'

'And I'm sorry too,' said Anne contritely. 'I should never have spoken to you like that, Mr. Bishop.'

'Not at all, Anne. In fact I admire how you defended Wally very much,' said Jeff, looking round the table at his employees now, 'In my position it is not very often that people have the courage of their convictions and speak out when I have said something wrong or offensive. I wish it would happen more often.'

There was an embarrassed silence for a few seconds until Steve gave a little cough, and said that perhaps it was time to continue to talk about delivery timings, which were under discussion before Mr Bishop joined the meeting.

-ooOoo-

Down on the beach Morgan was surprised to see so much activity.

There were diggers much in evidence and a great scar had been opened up in the beach where they had taken sand to 'blind' the base of his caravan park before they started filling the lagoon they had created with sewage.

Out in the sea itself, an enormous orange boom bobbed gently in the water, containing the raw sewage spill as far as was possible. Boats sprayed water, and huge pipes laid across the beach, presumably connected to unseen pumps, fought to remove the pollution from the sea.

Morgan could see another huge digger halfway up the cliff, where the little waterfall once played on the hard rocks below. There were several small tipper trucks on a makeshift road cut into the dunes and the digger was hard at work shovelling the mess out of the stream into them for disposal.

Morgan wondered where they were taking all the muck, but as he approached the sorry remains of his amusement arcade now, next to the boarded-up hotel, he had a better view of the huge deep trench they had dug to remove sand. There he could see the tipper trucks unloading and another digger, which was burying the result.

Morgan made a mental note to keep his grandchildren away from this beach even after the clean-up operation was complete.

As he glanced again at the black scar where the once very pretty stream flowed, he wondered if the local newspaper might be interested to know how they were disposing of the pollution, and he resolved to mention it to his neighbour, who worked part time in the newspaper office, when he saw him at Chapel.

-oo0Ooo-

THIRTY-FOUR

There was only the rather spartan Renault Kangoo van thing with the side windows available from the car club, so Tim had no option but to book it. He hoped Hazel wouldn't mind that it was rather basic and a bit noisy.

It was certainly not as comfortable as the Vauxhall Corsa he used before, or that Ford Focus that Hazel hired to drive them down to Wales, but there was no choice, so it would have to do.

There was a choice of rooms available at the Grand Hotel in Cromer, however, and having discussed it with the receptionist over the telephone, Tim spent an extra thirty pounds and booked the 'bridal suite' which apparently had the best view in the hotel and a little lounge area, as well as the bedroom and bathroom. The pictures on the internet the receptionist directed him to, also featured a four-poster bed and wide windows looking out to sea and across the famous Cromer pier.

Whilst politely refusing the hotel receptionists offer to put fresh flowers in the room, as he remembered Hazel's hay fever, he did allow himself to be talked into having Champagne on ice with two glasses placed in the room along with a bowl of fruit and some chocolates. Extravagant, it certainly was, but Tim was determined to make up for having to disappoint Hazel over their

Brighton trip, if he could.

A little more internet research revealed the existence of a rather smart restaurant in a country house about half a mile away from the hotel. Tim booked a table there without asking Hazel, when he saw Cromer crab on the menu. This establishment offered fine dining, in admittedly pricey but quite elegant surroundings, and he thought Hazel would be impressed if he kept it as a surprise.

Now quietly pleased with what he had done, Tim dialled Hazel's number to tell her some, but not quite all, of his arrangements, and to agree a time to pick her up early on Saturday morning.

-ooOoo-

'Considering,' said Steve. 'That went very well.'

'I have apologised,' said Anne. 'I just couldn't …'

'It really is fine, Anne,' said Wally. 'I actually think it may have increased Jeff Bishop's respect for you and demonstrated that we are a tight team.'

'If a little indisciplined,' said Anne.

'Never mind. We got through it and have a firm order for five units and a sixth on the way if they can sort out the problems on the Norfolk site. That is the real news,' said Steve.

'It was quite funny,' chuckled Wally.

'What was?' snapped Anne, bristling.

'That we know what is going to happen when the Minister gets to that site on Saturday, and Jeff Bishop and his cronies haven't got a clue,' said Wally.

'Oh that,' said Anne and occupied herself for most of the rest of the drive with her mobile phone, sending an email to Professor

Potts and another to Professor Misato Ho.

-ooOOoo-

'The problem seems to be with the Environment Agency people,' said Bethany Ford. 'As far as I can make out, Uncle Giles, they don't think the method you proposed for de-contaminating it works. That is why it was dropped out of the long list of sites.'

Giles Norton-Bunkerman sucked on his cigar, swore when he realised it had gone out, and tried to re-light it before he spoke.

'It's only a bit of creosote, for goodness sake Bethany, and frankly I was rather hoping that you would have a bit more influence, when we got you on the Government Commission and what-not.'

'We have been through this, Uncle Giles …'

'And after all the money I put up with Jacob Mortimer to get Amanda Trunnion elected, too …'

'You can't …'

'Yes, yes. I've heard it all before, Bethany. But everyone else does it, so why shouldn't I use my money to try to get things done how I want them?'

'In a democracy, Uncle Giles …'

'Pah! Democracy be damned! The shed business is losing money and I want to redevelop the site with some nice detached houses for the better sort of people to buy, start families and live their lives. The shed factory is noisy, and it stinks, and the locals all hate it and want to see it closed down, so how is that a bad thing? Pretty much promoting the will of the people, I'd say!'

Bethany raised her eyes to the ceiling. She had had this discussion so many times with her uncle, and his opinions would not be changed one little bit.

'I'm going to take the dogs for a walk before it rains,' she said.

'Take a shotgun, Bethany, and have a pop at some of those green haired, bleeding heart, unwashed environmental protesters by the main road. There seem to be more of them up there than ever … and now the hedgerows have gone, you can see the blighters from the billiard room windows, if you don't keep the blinds drawn. Awful!'

-ooOoo-

'By the weekend they will be pumping it out and into the silo at last, Ewan, man.'

'Great, isn't it, Dai. What a job those electrical guys did. So quick!'

'Especially as they had to spend the last few days sitting on their hands while the parts they needed were at the docks.'

'Maybe we will be free of these bloody flies soon too.'

'Well, I really do hope so. This has been awful.'

'I've even got them in my ruddy house right up on the top. Unhygienic that is.'

'Your house is miles away compared to mine, Dai, man. Imagine what it has been like in my place, by here. You can see my roof from the road outside, so that means the flies can see it too. Horrible it's been. Horrible.'

-ooOoo-

THIRTY-FIVE

Leaving his house in good time to get to the Constituency Surgery being held today in Cromer, Gordon Sparrow congratulated himself.

He was pleased that he had managed to persuade Tim to attend both the surgery and the meeting on the building site afterwards. His natural inclination was to offer the good fellow lunch after the site visit to thank him, but he remembered what Patrick Blenny had said about the inadvisability of entertaining the staff, so he hoped his sincere words of thanks would be enough.

The spectre of members of the media turning up at the building site was an all too real possibility, but with Tim alongside him he would feel much more confident in dealing with them. As far as he could make out, they were only likely to be local press. They would be there to see the inevitable handful of protestors complaining about more houses being built, so he did not allow himself to worry about it too much.

By the looks of things, there wasn't much on the agenda for him to deal with at the Constituency Surgery either. But these were open public meetings so one could never be sure who might wander in.

Gordon smiled as he remembered one of the early surgeries he held as a rookie MP, before he became a junior Minister. On that occasion, a local farmer, somewhat the worse for wear, had stumbled in and accused him of stealing his tractor. After some minutes the local Constable attending pointed out of the window of the pub where, on that occasion, the surgery was being held, and drew the farmer's attention to the fact that his tractor was parked outside. Then to the amusement of those present, he reminded the now embarrassed farmer that he had had a ride home in a police car late the night before, because he was not considered fit to drive. The tractor had been there all night.

There was always an element of uncertainty at these surgeries, but with nothing very contentious on the list of issues he had been given so far, Gordon did not allow himself to become too concerned about it.

-ooo0oo-

Until they discovered the dirty plastic compost bag under the back seat of the Renault Kangoo, as they stopped at the services near Stanstead, Tim and Hazel had not enjoyed their journey.

They had had to keep the windows open pretty much all the time which, considering most of the journey was on motorways, made it quite unpleasant.

Hazel was most definitely not happy, and until the empty bag was discovered, she had been exploring the topic of the inadvisability of hiring a vehicle, previously used by local gardeners to shift unpleasant smelling things about, from just about every imaginable angle.

With the bag removed and three car air-fresheners purchased at the motorway services positioned in the car, the journey did then become more bearable. Hazel stopped berating Tim about the smell and kept her discontented comments to other matters, such as the hardness of the seats and the uncomfortable jiggling the noisy little Renault produced at anything above about forty miles per hour.

Nerves were a little frayed, therefore, when they arrived at the Grand Hotel in Cromer to drop off their bags.

-oooOoo-

The journey to Norfolk was much less uncomfortable for Anne and Steve in his mum's elderly but serviceable BMW.

They had debated whether they should attend the meeting on site to see the Professor's 'protesters' strutting their stuff, and decided that it was too good an opportunity to miss. So long as they kept at a discrete distance from the action and stayed out of sight, it was worth the journey for the experience.

Having also learned that Gordon Sparrow, the MP now heading up the Government Commission which had started all this, was holding his regular Constituency Surgery in nearby Cromer, not that far from the site, and that his meeting was open to the public, they decided to stay in the seaside town. They would drop into the meeting to see what it was all about before driving to the building site for the main event.

Lacking the wherewithal to stay in a proper hotel like The Grand, Anne and Steve had booked themselves into a little boarding house, three rows back from the beach, promising bed and full English breakfast for the residents of each of the four letting rooms. As they tumbled up the narrow stairs past the chintzy curtains on the landing, following the robust and formidable looking landlady, they were informed that breakfast was at eight thirty sharp, and they were to leave their key on the hook inside the front door and be back in by eleven, if they went out.

As the faded glory of the room was revealed to them with a wave of her chubby arm, the landlady also informed them that pets and smoking were not allowed and that they were welcome to 'sit out' in the little garden at the back if they liked, so long as there were no ball games.

When the landlady departed and Steve, gingerly testing the bed, heard one of the springs twang, they both dissolved into fits of uncontrollable giggles. This was going to be a fun weekend.

-oooOoo-

THIRTY-SIX

'Oh Tim, it's lovely!' Hazel's scepticism had been dispelled, or at least put on hold, as she looked around the 'bridal suite' at the Grand Hotel. 'Look at the view!'

Tim was pleasantly surprised too.

Although, if one looked hard enough, it was easy to find corners where The Grand Hotel could do with a bit of a spruce up, the general ambience of the place was of comfortable, olde world charm. It may not have been The Grand Hotel in Brighton, but it certainly presented a pleasant enough prospect on the North Norfolk coast as some consolation.

'Timothy! Is that Champagne on the table, and chocolates too? You naughty boy, you are spoiling me.'

'Well, I ...'

'Bit too early to open it, maybe, and I suppose you will be wanting to get along to your Minister's meeting soon enough. But honestly Tim, this does almost completely make up for not going to Brighton.'

'I'm very glad you like it Hazel ...'

'So that only leaves me to devise a suitable punishment for the grimy compost bag ridden stinky old van … I'll have to give that one some serious thought.'

-oo0oo-

'To be honest,' said Steve, 'I found it rather boring.'

Anne and Steve had walked from their boarding house to the little hall for the Minister's Constituency Surgery, and were now walking back to get the car and travel to the building site near Norwich.

'Yes, I'm afraid so. But an interesting insight into what MPs have to do, though. Do you fancy getting fish and chips before we leave here?'

'Yes please!' said Steve.

'Well, if I have remembered what I read about this town correctly, down the road straight ahead of us, before you get to the sea, there is a fish and chip place called Mary Jane's which has quite a reputation. You can sit inside to eat it too.'

'Perfect,' said Steve. 'Let's go for it.'

-oo0oo-

'Everything in place, Edwin,' said Misato.

'Thank you, Misato. I hope it all goes to plan,' said the Professor. 'There was a time when I would have liked nothing more than to be there rubbing shoulders with the protesters, but I'm afraid those days are gone. I'm sure though that after your briefing, the young people will make an excellent job of it, and I look forward to hearing all about it.'

'We'll know soon enough. There is a live feed from one of their mobile phones available if you are interested …'

'Alas, Misato, it is my day to do the weekly shop, where I meet one or two people for coffee and a chat. I am due there shortly.'

'Edwin, you don't stop, do you. You are supposed to be retired, but I know all about this group you hold in the cafe in Tesco's discussing … now what was it? "The influence of history on modern politics and our lives today?" Isn't that your latest theme?'

'How ever did you hear about that?'

'Oh, word gets around. Your little classes are very popular it seems, particularly with the Tesco staff.'

'Well, it is just a little interest …'

'And I also hear the rumour that they looking to hire the Community Hall because the group is getting too big for the cafe …'

'Well, nothing is decided yet, but they have been very kind about it and …'

'And you gonna end up working full time again if you don't watch out!'

'No, no. It is nothing like that. I don't get paid for these friendly little get togethers, you know.'

'What time will you be finished? I'll ring you and let you know how it went on the building site.'

THIRTY-SEVEN

'Oh good grief!' said Tim as he hurried towards the Minister, who was surrounded by placard waving protesters.

'Now this is more like it!' said Hazel, setting her mobile phone to 'record'.

-ooOOoo-

'And then all hell broke loose, Professor,' said Anne breathlessly.

'The people from the National Grid who had been moaning about not having the resources or staff to speed up building the step-down transformer and sub-station, were pretty much chased off the site and had to make a run for it before the other protestors caught up with them,' added Steve, looking over Anne's shoulder into the FaceTime screen.

'The other protesters?' said the Professor.

'Yes. Not our lot. The ones who were just there to complain about houses being built generally,' explained Anne. 'It seemed Professor Misato's protestors did such a good job of convincing them, that they started shouting about wanting free electricity too.'

'So, they effectively switched sides!' Steve chuckled. 'It was wonderful to watch.'

'What did the Minister, Gordon Sparrow make of all this?'

'Well, at first he seemed a bit overwhelmed,' Anne explained. 'But his assistant, or whatever he was, kept whispering to him and after a while he got up quite a head of steam and started putting the electricity people ... National Grid, wasn't it? ... and started putting them on the spot about why they couldn't speed up building the new power station ...'

'Step-down transformer and sub-station, and it is National Grid and UK Power Networks,' corrected Steve.

'Step-down sub-station, sorry. Anyway, he started in on them about it and they bleated about not having the resources and enough trained operatives.'

'The Minister wasn't having any of that,' said Steve. 'He told them that the Government had asked for their support to build much needed new homes and they were letting the side down.'

'Yes. By this time a few more journalists and members of the public seemed to be turning up, and this assistant bloke, who was whispering to the Minister all the time seemed to come up with something really powerful.' Anne paused for breath. 'One of the journalists, a woman who hadn't said much up until this point stepped forward and asked him, the Minister, I mean, to confirm that this was one of the demonstration sites for the Government's programme which could see free green electricity made available, and in response he pretty much recited the first two pages of our proposal document! It was brilliant!'

'After that,' said Steve, 'everyone on site was gunning for the National Grid and UK Power Networks people and demanding to know what they were going to do about it. Then our protesters got up a bit of a chant.'

'Oh, Professor, you would have loved it. They were chanting

"Free power for all!" and "Bio-generators in every town. Now!" And believe it or not quite a few of the normal protestors joined in!'

-oo0Ooo-

Sir Jacob Mortimer sat back in the plush leather chair in his office in Holborn.

'I see, Jeff. Well, that does put a different complexion on it.'

'It does, doesn't it,' Jeff Bishop set aside his tea and leaned forward in his seat. 'This old Professor bloke, the one who wrote the introduction to the proposal for the Bio-digester turbines, has come up with a way to pretty much force the UK PowerNetworks people to get on with it.'

'What do we know about this proposal, Jeff?'

'I need to get my people to read all the guff he has produced properly, but the gist of it seems to be that if we are prepared to work jointly with National Grid or UK Power Networks, and the Government to set up and fund a training facility for people to learn how to work on the power networks, they agree to divert labour from other projects to get the transformer to feed the sub-station in Norfolk done, which will release the site for development.'

'Why on earth should you fund a training facility for them, Jeff?'

'Well, actually it could help us as well. This old Professor fossil has put up an idea that we could take over the old Building Research Establishment College, which closed a handful of years ago when the funding stopped. The National Grid and UK Power people could do their training there.' Jeff took a sip of his tea. 'In its heyday the college was a pretty big affair and offered apprentice training for brickies, plasterers, sparkies, and all that sort of thing. The power people won't need to use all of it, but this Professor bloke is asking if we would consider funding their bit, to get the transformer and sub-station built, and also use it to train up our own site people.'

'Intriguing. And how does that sit with you?'

'At first I thought it was boll ... er, I mean pie in the sky, but then I realised I could get all our subbies ... sub-contractors, that is, to pay for it to use to train up their apprentices. If we, and they, can show that we are offering training it always helps us get Local Authorities interested and softens them up a bit on our planning applications. Before it closed down, we used to send some apprentices to this college ourselves to achieve the same end.'

'I see,' Sir Jacob was becoming interested.

'And there is a bit more to it than that, you see. There are always delays with getting power to sites, either because of physical problems or just paperwork. But the top people at the power networks might be prepared to fast track our applications if we use a bit of political muscle to persuade them to keep training people at the college beyond just this Norfolk transformer and sub-station. Who knows, it could un-plug a load of things and give us and our subbies a bit more access to site labour along the way.'

'The fact that the Bio-digester turbines can put electricity back into the network, rather than just taking it out, could help with the political angle, perhaps.'

'It is a sort of a nice circle, don't you think? We get our planning consents to build people houses with Bio-digesters. Our buyers move in and shit, which creates the gas to drive the turbines, and in turn they pump any excess power they generate back into the network. The fact that we create green power gets the Planners all excited, and when we add in that we also train up the work force to build the houses as well as the power networks, offering local employment along the way, everyone is winning.'

'It sounds most agreeable.'

'Oh, and I forgot one bit. The company making the Bio-digesters and turbines will also be training people there to build, install and manage the things, so we, and they, create the capacity to install them wherever we need them.'

'That might link in neatly with the other little project we talked about privately, Jeff ...'

'What, buying out Bio-Power Solutions (Oxford) Ltd., you mean?'

'Yes, if we could do that, we could ensure that the units become available only for sites you are developing, and by cornering the market you control who can use them and where.'

'Which will potentially frustrate some of the other builders ...'

'And possibly force them to sell their land-banks ...'

'To us.'

'Precisely. More tea?'

-ooOoo-

THIRTY-EIGHT

'So Weasel-Face, I mean Hamish Glover, was having lunch with Kane Bois, the Education Minister …'

'Do you know him?' asked the Professor.

'No, not really. Rugby man, I think, and by all accounts a bit of a tic.'

'I'm sorry, Sebastian, I interrupted you, please continue.'

'No worries, Potty, old man. Now where was I … Oh yes. Hamish, I mean Weasel-Face, had Bois cowering and cringing, and by the looks of things agreeing to everything he wanted.'

'Which was?'

'Why, to back an apprentice education scheme for building trades at this college Hamish has being going on about. Didn't I explain that?'

'I'm sure you did. Please do go on.'

'Well, by the time they got as far as the port, Bois seemed to be completely under Weasel-Face's spell and was nodding and making notes on a napkin as to what he had to do. That was when the Home Sec., Lakshmi Prakash turned up with that dreadful oaf Giles Norton-Bunkerman. Or rather, not actually with him, just at the same time. It seemed Norton-Bunkerman had come to join Horrid, I mean Horace Smithson, the former Prime Minister, you know; while the Home Sec., had come to winkle out Weasel-Face and the Bois twerp and take them back for some important meeting at Number 10.'

'An interesting combination.'

'Yes. Well, I don't know if you are aware what a frightful uncouth thug this Norton-Bunkerman chap is, but absolutely without being invited, he plonked himself down at old Weasel-Face's table and started on about why his creosote works or some such couldn't be developed for housing. I didn't catch much of it, I'm afraid because my old pal Fish-Breath, I mean Reggie Gill, had turned up to take me off to a rather cosy gathering for a preview at a gallery in Knightsbridge, where we were the guests of Mrs Sylvia Pimmsol and her attractive daughter Angela. It was a bash I had rather been looking forward to, as a matter of fact, because this Angela had stated to Reggie in set terms that she hoped I would go along.'

'I see.'

'I hope that is a bit of a help, Potty, and I'm sorry I couldn't tell you any more of what transpired.'

-ooo0oo-

'Have you noticed the amount of rats running about by here, Dai?' asked Ewan.

'Well, you can't have sewers without rats, man, and there have always been rats around here.'

'True, but it seems that there are more about than usual.'

'I suspect that is because they found plenty of interesting things to eat when the old caravan park was being filled up, so they bred more. Their population will return to normal soon enough, and there are fresh traps down since the work finished. It won't be our problem soon though, Ewan, man.'

'So, you are going to Tenerife, then Dai. Very nice!'

'We have been to the other Canary Isles, so this will complete the set, if you like. What about you, Ewan?'

'Well, the original plan was two weeks in sunny Spain, but you know what my mother is like, so I'm off over to Cardiff again to stay with her and my sister. I don't mind, really. It will just be nice to get away from here for a spell.'

'Yes, it certainly will. I can't wait. And now that the re-commissioning is complete, and the plant is up and running again we can forget all about it for a while.'

'The only thing that bothers me about that, is it will have to run at almost full power while we are away and then for at least four weeks to clear up the backlog and start running normally. These temporary blokes coming in are going to have to keep a close eye on it …'

'I wouldn't worry, Ewan, man. They will have four days working alongside us first so, if they can't drive the thing after that, we have only ourselves to blame.'

'Blame ourselves?'

'Just joking, man. They will be fine. Although why they think it will take four blokes to do the job you and I do on our own, is beyond me.'

'Bit odd that. The management must have a different idea as to what happens here most of the time. But that is up to them, I suppose. Now then. Three across, "Antipodean flightless bird," three letters … any idea?'

-oo0Ooo-

Nigel Bannister had worked in the garden centre for a little over six years, with five of those years spent in the extensive 'water-gardens' section.

As Deputy Assistant Manager, particularly since the Assistant Manager went off on long term sick leave with stress, Nigel had been responsible for ensuring that stock levels were maintained and ordering in various items as needed. Now though, the water gardens were due to be comprehensively re-modelled, with new demonstration ponds and pools, holding tanks, landscaping and new areas for customers to see and choose live fish and water plants.

But although the refurbishment was long overdue there was a problem.

The plan involved the purchase of large quantities of rubberised plastic flexible pond lining, which would be used to contain the water in the new water gardens and ponds and also be sold, by the length, to those customers wishing to create their own water features at home. But it had emerged that there was a national shortage of this material.

None of their normal suppliers could help, and certainly could not supply in the quantities and quality required to complete the planned re-modelling scheme, so Nigel had to search the internet for a new source of the material.

Eventually, and largely by chance, he came across an advertisement for a quantity of a very similar material, which was actually rather more substantial than the stuff usually used for garden pond construction, but which would do admirably for their purposes. The advertisement, which Nigel scanned through rapidly in his excitement, explained that the material had been purchased for an environmental project and was now surplus to requirements. There was considerably more of it than they needed, but Nigel was so relieved to actually find some that he immediately ordered the entire stockholding to be delivered as soon as possible.

The purchase was made all the more attractive by the very reasonable price being asked, and as he glanced delightedly at the advert, it was the price in particular that caught Nigel's eye, and he did not hesitate to place his order.

Any of the product they did not use, Nigel reasoned, could be sold off to the public at a substantial profit, and as the quantities were so large, there might even be enough left to sell off to cover the initial cost of the entire consignment.

On the day that the material was due to be delivered, Nigel was delighted to open the gates for three large lorries to enter the yard and unload.

He should have been more observant and noticed that the vast rolls of black plastic were steaming slightly and that a cloud of flies seemed to be enveloping the yard, but when the Manager himself came out of his office and asked what on earth was causing that smell, Nigel, who had signed off the delivery and closed the gates after the departing trucks, at last stepped back to examine his purchase.

'Well, it said "shop soiled" on the advert,' bleated Nigel, before he was sent back to the office to find the advert and present it to the Manager in person.

'Nigel, you buffoon!' said the Manager, holding a handkerchief over his nose to mitigate the smell. 'This says "soiled," not shop soiled! You didn't read the advert properly. It says here it has come from an environmental project down in Wales somewhere, and had been used for a short period to contain fluid waste. We can't sell that! What the hell are we going to do with this stinking great lot of plastic!'

'Ah,' said Nigel; and as he examined the address on the delivery note he had signed before the lorries left, he realised that he recognised it as the holiday caravan campsite in Wales where he and Alison had had that disastrously curtailed holiday.

The pervasive smell in the yard was also all too familiar.

-ooo0oo-

The dinner at the country house restaurant was exquisite in every detail, but Tim and Hazel had to rush to get there in time for their table booking.

It took Hazel some time to write up and submit her story about the events on the building site, during which Tim, having dropped her at the hotel, had more work to do with the Minister at his private residence, over coffee, a few miles down the road.

By the time he got back to the hotel, there was only just time to change before they had to drive to the restaurant.

The slightly frazzled couple found it difficult to relax and enjoy their meal, which, given the quality of what they were being served was a great pity. Realising they were wasting a splendid and not inexpensive experience, they discussed repeating it at some future date, when they could devote themselves to savouring it better.

The champagne on ice in the room was now champagne in lukewarm water and they decided to take the bottle home with them and just eat the chocolates before collapsing, exhausted into bed.

-ooo0oo-

THIRTY-NINE

On receipt of the order, Ceylex Engineering began the process of gearing up to produce the pressurised mini-silos and the gas turbine units in quantity and at pace. They worked alongside Balance Electrical Systems who were involved in production of the wiring for the original scheme in Wales, and then the miniaturised plant in the gardens by the student accommodation where Wally Walters lived.

They welcomed Amy Scott and Ralph Tennyson to their factory. These two were Professor Potts' chosen graduates who would be joining the Ceylex payroll to undertake the role of training staff to maintain the units. Initially, they were there to observe the manufacturing process and oversee the installation of the first demonstration units.

The paperwork involved in granting Wally the original patent for his invention was extensive and had taken many months to negotiate, but now, a couple of years later, the Professor had arranged for the head of the Law Faculty at the University to rapidly draw up watertight licenses. These would ensure that those building, installing and maintaining the units were safeguarded and given the right to work on the units by the Company.

The Professor had previously arranged for Anne and Steve to create Bio-Power Solutions (Oxford) Ltd., as a stand-alone Company; and for the Memorandum and Articles to allow them to buy and sell shares, issue dividends and trade with the minimum of difficulty. He was eager to ensure that they had complete control of the company and could run it as they wanted.

As work started in the factory, Jeff Bishop's team confirmed that the first of the demonstration projects was to be installed on a site in Chessington, where Pomegranate Homes were building sixty-one houses and flats, and foundation works were underway. The unit was to be installed, as soon as possible, in an area designated to eventually become a children's play park when the scheme was complete.

Anne and Steve took Professor Potts to the former Building Research Establishment College to meet an architect, employed by Pomegranate Homes, who was tasked with remodelling the buildings where necessary to create or, in most cases re-create, facilities to train the likes of bricklayers, roofers, electricians, plasterers, painters, plumbers, and of course the operatives of the National Grid and UK Power Networks.

The college buildings had been empty for three or four years but, being in a relatively secluded rural location, they had suffered little damage. Apart from the inevitable graffiti on the perimeter walls and the collapse of a section of security fence, caused when squatters had tried to move in, but were quickly moved on, there was surprisingly little remedial work required to get the facility up and running again.

The architect pointed out that the building was adjacent to, and originally part of an RAF base, now used by the American Air Force, so there were plenty of security-conscious personnel about to keep an eye on it.

The main work, however, would involve refurbishing the somewhat battered accommodation blocks, where students on residential courses would stay. As residential building was the specialism of Jeff Bishop's group of companies, that element of the works was being left to Pomegranate Homes.

The Professor declared himself delighted with what he saw, and after their meeting with the architect finished, he suggested that they went to a local pub for lunch.

While they were ordering their food, the Professor received an email from Jeff Bishop confirming that he had just signed a ten-year lease with HM Government, in the form of the Ministry for Education, to take over the former Building Research Establishment College, which he announced was to be renamed 'The Pomegranate Homes Building Training College'. The email went on to ask if they could add words to the effect that it was being run in association with the University of Oxford somewhere in the title.

-ooo0oo-

FORTY

Philip Knowles from the Environment Agency, under pressure from Hamish Glover, agreed to write to Giles Norton-Bunkerman, to explain why the site of his shed factory was not considered suitable for development in relation to the proposal he had made.

He explained carefully, and given what he had been told about Giles Norton-Bunkerman, in simple language, that it was true to say that the little factory represented a 'non-conforming use in the Green Belt'. As such, it would be supported for re-development by the Local Authority as it meant the closure of the factory, but de-contaminating the site was not a straightforward or cheap process.

His letter stated that "Current Government guidance requires all proposed housing development sites, that are to be built on or near potentially or known contaminated land, to undergo a Preliminary Risk Assessment to identify the potential risk from land contamination. This assessment, on the site in question, is likely to conclude that further testing is needed in order to determine the levels of risk present at the new build site. This is the point when further investigation, usually some form of Intrusive Site Investigation, should be carried out for the proposed housing development." And so it went on, for eight close-typed pages.

'Well, Bethany,' Giles Norton-Bunkerman asked, when the letter arrived, 'What do you make of that?'

'It will cost a fortune,' said Bethany. 'And of course you will be expected to pay for it, Uncle Giles.'

'What I can't see,' said Giles, throwing the stub of his after-lunch cigar into the fireplace, 'is why, if the Government are so desperate for new houses and so short of land to put them on, why they won't pay for all this Investigation and Assessment and all that waffle. Makes no sense to me.'

'No. Well, there it all is Uncle Giles. Eight pages of reasons and explanations.'

'From a bloody Civil Servant, who I'm paying to prat about writing novels saying why not, rather than being positive and offering solutions. They will turn my hair white.'

'You already have grey hair, uncle.'

'Well, make what hair I have drop out then! Bah! I only want to build fourteen or fifteen nice big detached four-bedroom houses in quarter acre plots with double garages and what-not. Surely that is not too much to ask.'

'Perhaps you would have more luck if you suggested building affordable social housing on the site …'

'What! Council houses! And have glorified benefit scroungers in the village! I should never hear the last of it! Maybe I would just be better to knock the bloody factory down and plant sugar beet on it.'

'I don't think …'

'Pah! I'm going to see how Bert is getting on spraying off all those ruddy weeds on the old water-meadow, down by the river. I want that ready for ploughing next month. Set-aside and wild flowers, be blowed! If it has to be designated as farmland, it should be producing a cash crop for me!'

Once again, as she heard the door of his Range Rover slam, Bethany raised her eyes to heaven. Trying to get her Uncle Giles to take any notice of any opinion other than his own had always been like this. She didn't think there was any point in trying to change him now.

-oo0Ooo-

The confirmations about the building sites were coming in thick and fast now.

Pomegranate Homes confirmed the details of three more of the demonstration sites. One, just outside Peterborough, was likely to be the second to be ready to receive the bio-digester and turbine, with occupations of the initial phase of houses expected imminently.

Now, with five out of the six proposed demonstration sites ready to go, and planning consents being negotiated, at last, on several of the sites on the so called 'long list', Jeff Bishop asked Sir Jacob Mortimer if he thought the time was right to make their approach to Bio-Power Solutions (Oxford) Ltd.

'Yes, Jeff. I think so. I can arrange to meet Professor Potts and sound him out next week if you like. I assume you would like to keep the identities of our little consortium private at this stage.'

'I think it would be wise, Sir Jacob. That old Professor is not daft and will obviously realise I'm involved to some degree, but he doesn't need to know who else is behind this just yet.'

'If at all. No doubt the longer we keep certain names out of it the better it will be.'

'Indeed so.'

-oo0Ooo-

Steve and Anne took Wally to meet Amy and Ralph at the Ceylex engineering factory in time to see the first bio-digester mini silo casing coming off the production line. Wally was impressed.

'When we did the first one for the student accommodation, it was a much more haphazard affair,' he said. 'More like men in sheds with hammers than this sleek production line. This is great!'

Amy and Ralph had prepared a little presentation which they asked if Wally would mind watching. The short video, and talk they had prepared was, they explained, what they were working on to use to present details of the process and the equipment to operatives. They were also going to adapt their double act for purchasers of new houses and create a video of it so that the new homes sales people could show it to prospective buyers.

Having watched it, Wally had a few technical comments to offer and Anne suggested that Ralph in particular needed to look into the camera more, rather than at his script.

'But the content is great and it flows very nicely,' said Steve. 'It might be worth producing another version of it to act as a Press Release that the media could use to advertise the scheme in 'advertorials' and perhaps even offer to local TV news companies in the locations where the demonstration projects are being built.'

'And if you incorporate a little more of the maths to demonstrate how, once it is up and running, it can create effectively free electricity, that is bound to get everyone excited,' added Anne.

Amy and Ralph had been making notes and promised to send each of the presentations round for comment when they had prepared them. They were, they said, very excited by the opportunity they had been given and asked if the visitors could convey their thanks once again to Professor Potts.

-ooOoo-

FORTY-ONE

'Well, yes, there are quite a lot of rats, so I'd still keep the doors shut by here,' Dai was saying. 'But at least the swarms of flies have gone since the old quarry was decommissioned and the temporary wall taken away. You don't know how lucky you are.'

Ewan and Dai were saying their last farewells to the four engineers who would be running the plant in shifts in their absence.

The three men and one woman had rapidly understood the process of running the facility and Ewan had expressed his confidence in them as he and Dai let themselves out of the control room and prepared to leave for their respective holidays.

'That Eva, she is quite something, don't you think, Dai? When we get back do you think she might let me take her out for a drink or something?'

'Put your tongue away, Ewan, man. She is a big city girl. Comes from up Swansea way. What would she want with a couple of blokes from the valleys like us.'

'Oh, I dunno,' said Ewan. 'I got the distinct impression that she was checking me out yesterday.'

'She was probably checking her escape routes as you were leering at her so much, more like!'

'We'll see, Dai, man. We'll see.'

-ooOOoo-

'So, lunch with the Home Sec., today,' Gordon reminded himself, 'and that internet link Tim gave me about understanding French menus was very useful.'

When Lakshmi Prakash, the Home Sec., had instructed her private secretary to invite Gordon Sparrow and Hamish Glover to Osbert's Club for lunch, it was with the intention of congratulating them on their work with the bio-digester turbines.

Gordon had shown himself to be very capable with the Press, according to the reports she had received following that little demonstration in Norfolk, and she decided it was time she got to know him better. He was certainly shaping up much better than that idiotic Trunnion woman, and she had high hopes for this project, and for the Commission he had taken over, about which she wanted to know more.

-ooOOoo-

'Well, please let me know what you think when you have sounded it out with your people, Professor. But can I just stress the importance of our conversation remaining entirely confidential. At this stage discretion is most important, and we would not want to do anything to disrupt the excellent progress being made.'

'Of course, Sir Jacob. I quite understand,' The Professor held open his front door for Sir Jacob to pass through. 'And have no fear, I shall be in touch quite soon.'

-ooOoo-

Hazel rarely visited the office behind Canary Wharf where her boss held court. With modern methods of communication, it was not necessary, and her editor took the view that, as an experienced journalist, with a lucky habit of being in the right place at the right time, she was quite capable of managing her own diary.

Today, however, she had wanted to see her boss on a private matter, and that was better done face to face.

Hazel had known Charlie Wright for the best part of fifteen years and their relationship was more one of equals than employee and employer. Charlie knew Hazel as a capable, organised and diligent reporter and an intelligent and generous friend.

He had often wondered why she was still single. She was certainly not unattractive, and with a lively intellect and a great sense of fun, he thought she would make someone a lovely wife.

She had been out to the house in Farnham several times and got on well with Fiona and the boys, as well. Although when they had invited her over for get-togethers of one sort or another, she had always come alone.

Fiona's attempts to pair her up had never worked either, and while she was always polite and charming, nothing ever came of that sort of thing.

What Hazel had to tell him today, therefore, was something of a surprise. He was delighted for her, of course, but he had not expected such news and was still trying to take it in.

Hazel was proposing to move in with her new boyfriend somewhere in the suburbs and wanted a salary increase to cover the railway season ticket costs she would incur.

-ooOoo-

FORTY-TWO

The next complete set had left the factory ready to be delivered to one of the demonstration sites.

Those already on site in Peterborough and Chessington were being installed, and Amy and Ralph had visited each site in turn to oversee the installation. They knew they would have to return when the first of the units was ready to be commissioned, and given the pace at which work was progressing, Amy was at pains to ensure that the van they were using was kept constantly filled up with fuel.

The news that work on the site just outside Norfolk was also about to start, now that the nearby transformer and substation had become such a hive of activity, with workers swarming all over it to get the construction work finished, was also received with excitement at the factory.

The new order to supply to that site meant that the production line did not have to be shut down and then restarted, and that meant a great deal to Ceylex Engineering and their cashflow.

-oo0Ooo-

'This is something of a shock, Professor,' said Steve.

'It is a lot of money,' exclaimed Anne. 'We could pay off all three of our student loans and still have enough left over for the deposit on a house!'

'And buy a car.'

'Or invest enough money to not have to worry about jobs for several years,' said Wally.

'It is certainly a surprise,' said Anne. 'I've only just sent out the first three invoices from the company ... Were you expecting anything like this, Professor?'

'Well, I did have an inkling that something like this might happen, but not quite so quickly. I should have realised that property developers like Jeff Bishop want to influence their destiny as much as possible and have control of as many elements of their business as they can.'

'So, you think he is involved in this then, Professor?' Steve asked. 'You said Sir Jacob Mortimer is representing a consortium of investors.'

'I am convinced that Jeff Bishop is one of this consortium, certainly,' smiled the Professor. 'Although, when I asked, Sir Jacob would not be drawn on who was behind this offer to buy out Bio-Power Solutions (Oxford) Ltd.'

'What do you think we should do?' Anne said.

-oo0Ooo-

'It was just Weasel-Face and that Jeff Bishop chap, and it was difficult to hear what they were saying because they were speaking very quietly. Scheming, I'd say.'

'I see, Sebastian. Did you manage to catch any of their conversation?'

'Not much, Potty old man. Except, as I was saying, when Hamish exclaimed that he had not expected quite such a high price to be offered initially, and complained that that left them little room to negotiate. I don't know if that is helpful?'

'Very helpful indeed, Sebastian. Thank you very much.'

-ooOoo-

Charlie Wright shook his head as Hazel left the office.

He knew she was determined and headstrong, but when he asked when she proposed to move in with this boyfriend, he was taken aback when Hazel said that the boyfriend didn't know anything about it yet.

'You mean to say it is not fixed up,' he had asked.

'No. He hasn't asked me to move in yet, but he will shortly,' Hazel had replied. 'And when he does, I shall accept and pack my bags.'

'So, this is just speculation then?'

'Oh no, not at all. It is all planned out.'

'But only by you at this stage …'

'Yes, Charlie. That is why I want to get this pay rise organised now so that I'm prepared to act.'

Charlie had given her the pay rise.

-ooOoo-

FORTY-THREE

Kenneth Jones MS sat in his office in the Senedd Cymru building in Cardiff and opened the draft report.

It was the preliminary findings of the investigation into the causes of the original explosion at the bio-digester and turbine plant and even just the 'Executive Summary' made interesting reading.

It transpired that the cause of the explosion was nothing to do with bad workmanship or poor design at the EU funded plant itself, but was simply because there was a small electrical fire at the caravan camp site in the quarry which had ignited a cloud of methane escaping from a leak in the sewer feed pipe. That explosion had ripped apart the metal pipe, part of which had punctured the main silo and caused the second explosion there.

The report summary mentioned that there had been some history of a rat infestation at the caravan site which the operator had been struggling to get under control for some months before the explosion. It offered conjecture that if rats had gnawed the live electrical cable feeding the only touring caravan on site at the time of the explosion, that could have caused the initial electrical fire which ignited the methane cloud.

Kenneth Jones laughed out loud as he laid the report aside,

before calling in his secretary and asking her to make sure that Hamish Glover MP, the English Minister for the Environment, amongst other things, got a copy of the report with his compliments.

A second thought occurred to him, and he called her back and asked her to issue another copy to Amanda Trunnion MP at the same time.

-ooo0ooo-

'Of course, what they want is to own the patent to the process and design, rather than the company as such,' said the Professor. 'That is really a matter for Wally given that he owns the patent.'

'I don't really see it like that,' said Wally. 'Without the company set up and all the work Anne and Steve put into that, the original input of Professor Misato, and of course your inspiration and guidance, Professor, this would have just remained as an idea. We all own this, not just me.'

'That is a very generous and statesmanlike response, Wally,' said the Professor. 'Considerable effort has gone into this, and although my own minimal input is broadly irrelevant, I agree that Anne and Steve must be involved in making the decision as to how to respond to this.'

'I was hoping it would represent the start of a career for all of us,' said Steve. 'Although now I come to think about it, once it was up and running and became a mainstream building product, it would just be something requiring a process to be managed, rather than anything particularly creative.'

'I guess this is the hard end of business and commerce,' said Anne thoughtfully. 'Businesses and inventions get bought and sold every day, I suppose, although I am surprised this has happened now. I would have thought we would have had a few years to set it up and get it running before we had to face anything like this.'

'What do you want to do, Wally?' asked Steve.

'I felt protective of my work and the patent initially,' said Wally. 'But quite honestly, I take Steve's point that running a business process is not as attractive as the creative end of things. I think that if the Professor thinks this is a genuine approach, and unless he advises against it of course, then I vote to sell it.'

'That is what we need,' said Anne. 'We need to vote on it, if we think we have given it enough thought, and I propose that Professor Potts should have a vote too, given his input and the respect we all have for him.'

'You are too kind, Anne,' smiled the Professor. 'But if you give me a vote, I shall abstain. This has always been about you and the other young people, not about me at all. There is no rush to make this decision either, so can I suggest that you all sleep on it and if you feel you are ready tomorrow or perhaps the next day, then vote on it.'

'How do you feel, Anne,' asked Wally. 'Running companies and things like that seems so much like your destiny, and I know it is what you want to do, so do you really want to give this up for a bit of money?'

'It's an awful lot of money actually. More than any of us could hope to earn in the normal run of things in several years if we just had to go and get jobs,' replied Anne. 'I've been asking myself if we would be likely to get such an opportunity to get our hands on so much money ever again.'

'The other thing,' said Steve, glancing at the faces of his friends, 'is that we don't know if the business would succeed. We are so inexperienced and unsure about it all, and were it not for the Professor we would probably never have dared do anything like this. Maybe we should regard this as a golden opportunity and use some of the money to grow something else.'

'Like my smelly mobility scooters,' laughed Wally.

'Like your currently smelly, but shortly to be ... to be ... not smelly, and highly saleable ...' said Anne.

'And who knows what other indispensable inventions such vibrant and creative people will come up with in the future,' smiled the Professor. 'It is not for me to say, but perhaps you could consider setting some of the money aside to back projects and ideas others in our little group of thinkers might come up with from time to time.'

'I think that is exactly what we should do, Professor. We have gained valuable experience from this regarding setting up companies, getting patents, marketing, and all sorts. We could offer that knowledge base to really help others get entrepreneurial schemes off the ground.' Anne looked round the room. 'I've made up my mind. I vote we sell and set up a working fund with half the money to invest in new things.'

'Perfect,' said Steve. 'That gets my vote too!'

'And mine!' said Wally.

'And had I decided to vote after all, that would have got my vote as well,' said Professor Potts, beaming at his protégés.

-oooOoo-

FORTY-FOUR

Sir Jacob Mortimer admitted that, in anticipation of a positive response, he had already instructed his lawyer to draw up a draft contract for the acquisition of the company and the patent, which is why the sale went through so quickly. It helped that the Director of the Faculty of Law at the University was acting for the Company, and the thing was done in a matter of hours.

As he ended the call, the Professor slipped his mobile phone into the pocket of his old patched corduroy trousers and went to pull the first of his carrots. He hoped the young people liked carrot cake and that they would consider it suitable for a celebratory tea now that the sale of the business had gone through.

-oo0Ooo-

On the weekend that Wales won the Rugby World Cup and the celebrations caused the tills of the curry houses and kebab joints to jingle late into the night, long after the pubs had shut, Eva knew what was about to happen.

The plant was already running at pretty close to full capacity to clear the backlog in the holding tank, but after a full week of that, as the volumes started to increase when the effects of the Rugby World Cup victory began to show themselves in the pipeline, Eva turned everything up to the maximum and the plant ran as never before.

In Cardiff, having celebrated almost as much as any other patriotic Welsh rugby fan, Ewan sat just out of the hot September sun on his mother's patio. He was wearing sunglasses, although not because of the bright sunshine, and trying to steel himself to get up and make a fresh cup of strong black coffee. His mind was too preoccupied to give work a second thought. All he wanted now was quiet and coffee.

'Oh my God, Ewan! Come here quick and look at this!'

His mother's voice calling urgently from the house startled him, and despite the searing pain in his head as he moved, Ewan hurried into the lounge where his mother was watching the morning news on the television.

Ewan winced as the over-bright screen showed a reporter, and then, as the camera panned round, an enormous structure like a brown boiled egg with a ragged edge where the top had been sliced off. It was billowing clouds of smoke.

Ewan recognised it at once, of course.

The explosion had blown the top clean off the silo, the reporter was saying, and debris had been found up to a mile away.

A traffic warden had been lucky to escape with cuts and bruises when an enormous piece of metal fell onto the car he was in the process of booking and destroyed it totally, and a woman pegging out washing was frightened out of her wits when a substantial quantity of what appeared to be partly treated sewage landed on her greenhouse and several other gardens in a town half a mile from the plant.

As the reporter excitedly began to describe the effects several tons of flying debris had had on the fortunately empty village hall and adjacent chapel, nearer the plant itself, Ewan rifled through the pockets of his jacket, hanging, since last night, on the back of one of the dining chairs, in search of his mobile phone.

-ooOoo-

Dewi Davis from the Aberystwyth Argus was one of the first reporters on the scene and he was kind enough to call Hazel Trigg to alert her as to what was going on.

Hazel had given him a plug in one of her articles about the original explosion at the plant and now he was able to return the favour.

'Bladdy horrible mess, it is, Hazel. Much worse than last time. The whole lot has blown up by here. I'd be surprised if they can rebuild it this time. I reckon this is the end for this place.'

'Has anyone any idea what caused it this time?' Hazel asked.

'Well, nothing official like, but I've been chatting to Bryn, one of the fire service people. Known him for years, I have, so it was good to catch up.' Dewi gave a little cough. 'Don't half stink here, Hazel … anyway, as I was saying; Bryn said when they got in to the main silo there was this big control panel of wires and that sort of thing and it was all burned out. Bryn reckons that might have been the start of the fire that caused the explosion. Electrical like.'

'I see,' said Hazel.

'Bladdy hell! There's another one!'

'What's happened?'

'Rats! Bladdy big ones too ... There's dozens of them running about all over the site. Proper made me jump that one did. Almost ran over my foot!'

-ooOoo-

'Shit!' said Hamish Glover.

'Yes and plenty of it, sprayed liberally over half of Wales by the sound of it,' said Lakshmi Prakash the Home Secretary. 'You realise what this means, of course.'

'Probably that there will be such a wailing and a gnashing of teeth about the thing exploding again, that the Press will start saying the mini bio-digester turbines are not safe ...'

'And of course we shall have to ban them immediately for use on English building sites.'

'Rats,' said Hamish.

'Pardon me?'

'Sorry, Home Sec., I said rats ... I've just had a draft report through on what caused the first explosion at the plant in Wales. It contains conjecture that a small electrical fire caused by rats gnawing wires ignited the escaping gas, which exploded.'

'Very interesting, Hamish. But returning to my original point, will you arrange to draw up the necessary paperwork and Press Releases to confirm that these mini bio-digester turbine things are banned with immediate effect?'

'Yes, Home Secretary,' said Hamish sheepishly.

'Will you, and your little band of adventurers, lose a lot of money following your acquisition of the patent and the company making them, Hamish?'

'How ... How did you know about that? 'coughed a startled Hamish Glover.

'Oh, you know, I have my sources, 'smiled the Home Secretary. 'Ah good, there is Sebastian Burleigh-Marks over by the bar.'

'Oh, 'scowled Hamish. 'He used to call me Weasel-Face at school.'

'So you know him? 'she stated. 'A very useful chap to know. Hazel Trigg from The Gazette introduced me to him.'

'I see, 'said Hamish, as he realised where the Home Sec., had got her information.

'You will have to excuse me Hamish, I am due to meet him and Gordon Sparrow with his senior Civil Servant chap. Then we are due to meet Professor Edwin Potts and Hazel Trigg over at the Carlton Club. We are going to discuss the launch of this scheme to provide "bio-powered" mobility scooters for disabled people. It just might be the vote catching push our new "green agenda" needs...'

Thank you for reading this book, now here is an extract from **'Double Life Insurance'**, *Bob Able's lighthearted but fast moving thriller:-*

Chapter 1

Martin Dartnell-Parkes had been with Stiffhams Estate Agents, Surveyors and Auctioneers for nine weeks, and been paid twice already.

It was only the basic salary at this stage, but when the sales started coming through, Mr. Brownlow, the Branch Manager, had said they would see about putting him on commission. Even so, having an actual salary was a terrific novelty for Martin who, having just left school, had never had such riches in his life.

His mother had got him the job of course, through her contacts at the golf club, but Martin had managed to hush that up, so far at least, and he had begun impressing his growing circle of friends with his generosity at the local bar.

He was excited for the future and today his training took another step forward when Mr. Brownlow took him to measure up a house for the first time, to put it on the market.

Martin knew the owner of the house in question slightly. She helped out at the school library sometimes and would probably remember him, he thought.

Sylvia Pendle was something of a mysterious woman to Martin and his school friends. She was tall and bony, with wild hair of an indeterminate colour and pale grey penetrating eyes that seemed to be staring straight through you. She habitually wore billowing translucent dresses which always seemed to be pale grey.

Miss Pendle, as Martin knew her, was some sort of artist, or was she a writer? He couldn't be sure. When she helped out in the school library, she gave a literary appreciation class thing for sixth formers who were interested, alongside Mr. Jenkins, the Head of English.

Not being compulsory, Martin never bothered with those of course, so he had no first-hand knowledge of what she did there.

He did know she was recently divorced and now wanted to sell her house to move to some kind of commune in Wales. Martin thought it was all rather hippy.

Mr Brownlow parked his smart BMW just around the corner from Miss Pendle's house, explaining that it didn't do to be ostentatious with clients who were in what he called "straightened circumstances".

Martin had only a vague grasp of what that meant and no experience of life for people who did not fit into his parents' comfortable style of living. He knew there were poor people, of course, but he didn't think he had ever met one.

He wondered if Sylvia Pendle got paid to work at the school library, now that she was clearly beyond retirement age, and if she had to live on what she earned there.

The house they had come to see was an end of terrace. Quite modern, and rendered on the outside in a sort of pale grey colour which, Martin thought, was very similar to the floaty dresses Miss Pendle wore. The grey was relieved by a very bright green door framed by wind chimes and a fluffy 'dream catcher' thing which flopped about in the wind.

When Miss Pendle opened the door, she seemed even thinner than he remembered and was wearing her usual opaque pale grey wrap-around dress.

When her eye came to rest on Martin he realised, to his horror, that he had been staring at her breasts which, with the light coming from behind her, were quite visible through the material.

Martin blushed to the roots of his gingery hair and stammered out a 'Good morning', before dropping the pen he had been told to hold and almost losing his grip on the blue plastic clipboard which was part of the essential paraphernalia of his new trade.

Now invited into the lounge, Martin and Mr. Brownlow looked around.

Martin was vaguely aware that there was virtually no furniture in the room, just a low wide chair with thin, uncomfortable-looking, grey foam cushions, a glass coffee table, several bookcases, and some bits of bamboo in a big flowerpot beside the arch that led to the dining area. What he could not fail to notice, however, was the enormous impressionistic painting on one wall; and what it depicted shook Martin to the core.

It was a stylised view of a big white sofa with a long, stick-thin female form stretched out on it. This female was quite naked and as Martin's gaze reached the head end of the picture he caught sight of the penetrating pale grey eyes and realised, to his horror, that the artist's model was none other than Miss Sylvia Pendle, one time library assistant at his old school!

Mr Brownlow was prattling on about the state of the market and seemed quite unperturbed by the giant overbearing artwork, but Miss Pendle looked at Martin just as he looked away from it, and a slight knowing smile crossed her face.

Martin shuddered and hoped she hadn't noticed.

Before they arrived, Mr. Brownlow had explained the form which was now held in the clipboard under Martin's increasingly sweaty arm. It was a series of 'tick boxes' and little spaces for comments which it was Martin's job to fill in.

Martin had to mark things like the sink in the kitchen (single drainer - tick - stainless steel - tick - mixer taps - tick) and count the eye-level cupboards and base cupboards and write down an answer.

While Mr. Brownlow kept up his description of how Stiffhams would offer the house for sale and how it would be advertised and so on, Martin was dispatched upstairs to fill in the second part of his form, which involved counting wardrobes and radiators and that sort of thing.

The stairs rose to a little half-landing from the small hallway which, Martin noticed, was painted entirely in white, as were all the rooms he had seen so far. Other than the ghastly thing filling one wall in the lounge, there were no other pictures and somehow Martin felt that although the day was quite warm, this house had a bit of a chill to it.

As he turned the corner and arrived at the first-floor landing Martin noticed, and ticked the box for the loft access hatch, and opened the first door on his left.

This was the smaller of the two bedrooms with a window looking towards the road and Martin was surprised to see that it contained no furniture at all except a long, wide, white sofa. The very same sofa which appeared in the enormous painting downstairs.

Having ticked his boxes, Martin rapidly moved on to the next door, which was the unremarkable workmanlike bathroom, relieved only by every surface being covered by little bottles and pots containing all sorts of lotions and potions, interspersed by several partly burnt candles.

Martin ticked his boxes and moved on to the next room.

This, of course, was the 'master bedroom' in Estate Agent speak, and Martin cringed when on the wall behind the bed, a smaller, and mercifully less revealing version of the picture downstairs smote his eye.

At least, this time the model was draped in a bathrobe, but those penetrating eyes were now in a face that had the same slightly terrifying smile Miss Pendle had given him in the lounge.

The awful painting seemed to hold a message for him, saying it was all right to look; so Martin concentrated hard on his tick boxes and tried not to glance at it again.

The final door on the landing was just at the top of the stairs and to open it Martin had to move a small chair out of the way.

There wasn't much space between this door and the stairs and it opened outwards so Martin had to step backwards towards the top step to open it. The door was tight in its frame and Martin had to give it quite a tug to get it to open.

As it came open, with something of a rush, everything seemed to happen at once.

With a screech, an enormous tabby cat shot out of the cupboard at about the level of Martin's face and an avalanche of blankets and pillows and clothes burst from the shelves.

Martin stepped back, missed his footing on the top step and fell helter-skelter down the stairs.

The noise, of course, brought Miss Pendle and Mr. Brownlow running, and as they arrived Martin, though dazed, saw that he still had his pen clutched firmly in his hand.

All down the wall in great arcs perfectly describing his fall, there was now a line of blue ink on the otherwise unmarked paintwork.

The blankets, pillows and clothes had served to break Martin's fall to some extent and apart from a few bruises to his pride, Martin was pretty much undamaged.

Of the tabby cat, that actually lived next door, little more can be said. It charged into the lounge as Mr. Brownlow and Miss Pendle came out and presumably shot out of the cat-flap in the kitchen that Martin had so assiduously noted on his form.

As Mr. Brownlow and Miss Pendle helped him to his feet, however, he could not take his eyes off the pen-line all down the wall and he burned with embarrassment as he stammered out an apology .

Miss Pendle saw what he was looking at, and in the long seconds that followed, Martin and Mr. Brownlow stood and stared.

Then quite suddenly Miss Pendle threw back her head and released a throaty, rolling laugh that shook the walls and was so infectious and went on for so long that Mr. Brownlow soon joined in. Even Martin managed an embarrassed sheepish grin before remembering his manners and offering to clean up the damaged wall himself, if Miss Pendle would find that sufficient recompense for his clumsy accident.

As they were leaving, Miss Pendle explained that the enormous tabby cat liked to use this house as its headquarters when its own people were at work and loved to sneak into the airing cupboard to snooze in the warm, especially in the winter months. She went on to say that she had not seen the cat for several days and wondered how long it had been there.

That mystery was to remain unresolved, however, as Mr. Brownlow having finished photographing the house, packed away his cameras and made ready to leave.

-oOo-

The estate agent's window, set as it was in a little parade of shops just off the high street, saw only limited footfall.

Those who did stop were usually either genuine buyers or husbands waiting for wives visiting the dress shop next door.

One such husband was Geoffrey. His interest, however, was piqued by a photograph in the window of one of those houses on that popular estate that he had always rather liked.

'New on,' the banner across one corner of the picture proclaimed, and Geoffrey's eye took in 'immaculate order, large garden, garage and driveway' in the effusive description.

Geoffrey glanced through the window of the dress shop.

As far as he could make out, his wife must be in the fitting room, so would be ages yet.

He grasped the handle of the estate agent's door and stepped inside.

Steve had been watching Geoffrey from his desk inside the office and the view afforded between the plastic picture-hangers of the street outside enabled him to form an opinion of those who looked in the window or, when nobody was there, to watch the pretty girls on their way to the railway station beyond.

Steve thought that Geoffrey looked harassed. One of those men with domineering wives who made their lives a misery, he thought.

'Good morning,' he said as Geoffrey edged furtively through the door.

-oOo-

Of course, with no driving licence, let alone a car, Martin could not drive the customers around himself yet, as Steve and his other colleagues might. But sometimes Martin got to accompany potential buyers in their own cars.

Steve thought that was handy, especially if he wanted to be on his own in the office, as sometimes suited him.

Martin sat uncomfortably in the back of Geoffrey's car as Geoffrey's wife roundly told him off for wasting her time. She did not want to view houses, she informed him, and was annoyed that he had 'high-handedly' made this appointment. It was too late now, they were nearly there, but Geoffrey cowered over the steering wheel and Martin squirmed on his seat as the tirade went on.

Strictly speaking, Steve did not need to send Martin or anyone from the offices of Stiffhams Estate Agents to accompany viewers to 2 Easton Drive. The vendor there was quite happy to show people round and perfectly capable of dealing with Geoffrey and his hectoring wife, but Steve and Martin were on their own in the office this morning and Steve seized the opportunity to be completely alone to make a furtive telephone call and make plans with Rosalind, while her husband was at work. Martin did not know Steve's motivation, of course, and in his keen way he was just delighted to be doing something to help a possible sale.

When they arrived, Martin introduced everyone and started the house tour with an obvious and unnecessary observation that this was the entrance hall.

Geoffrey looked at his wife and then, when he was sure she wasn't looking at him, he glanced again at Janet. He liked what he saw very much indeed.

Miss Janet Bassett BDS, MSc was, to Geoffrey's eyes at least, absolutely gorgeous.

Her lustrous brown hair, large bright eyes and incredible smile reminded some people of a faithful Labrador, but to Geoffrey she was adorable in a quite different way.

When she smiled, her perfect teeth glowed as if she had swallowed a pocket torch and were the result of a considerable investment which, even at staff rates, came at an eye-watering price. The dental practice where Janet worked, however, were justifiably proud of their efforts and regularly produced Janet as an example of what they could achieve to customers. She had even been professionally photographed and most of her face now graced the practice's printed advertising material.

To Geoffrey, quite unaware of all this dental work, she was just about flawless, and he was having trouble dragging his eyes from her long enough to give 2 Easton Drive the attention it deserved.

Not so Geoffrey's wife, whose critical eye took in every detail of the house, and was not particularly impressed.

As Martin's unnecessary comments explaining the function of each room lagged just a little behind the rapid inspection she was giving it, before she moved on, it was obvious that she wanted the viewing over and done with as quickly as possible, so she could return to berating her husband for wasting her time.

Martin was not immune to the tension in the air. He saw and understood the disinterest Geoffrey's wife was exhibiting as his hopes for a share of Steve's commission on the sale were dashed. But he also noticed something else.

Geoffrey was gazing at Janet and to his surprise, Janet was returning his stare with little smiles and exhibiting a slight blush around the temples.

Martin had seen that sort of thing between boys and girls at his school and had a fair idea what it meant, so teaming up with Geoffrey's wife now, he hurried the house inspection on and bought the visit to a conclusion as fast as he could.

The journey back to the office to drop Martin off was conducted in a sort of strained silence.

Martin hopped out of the car and with only the minimum of polite comments and scuttled back into the office as soon as they arrived.

'Well,' said Steve, 'What happened?'

-oOo-

Rosalind realised she had been very foolish, of course.

She should never have encouraged Steve, and now she was finding it hard to shake him off.

He may be tall and handsome and certainly charming, but she was happily married, wasn't she? All right, she and Mike had been having this on-going rumbling row for about six weeks now, and she couldn't even remember what started it, but harsh words had been exchanged and sniping, niggling comments had coloured their conversations ever since.

Mike was great though. Solid dependable Mike. Straightforward uncomplicated Mike. Whatever was the matter with her? Why on earth had she allowed Steve to buy her that drink? It was foolish and impulsive and, although that was as far as it went, Steve obviously thought she was still interested and was pushing to take her out to dinner and God knows what.

Even if she wanted to, how on earth could she do that? She had Mike's supper to cook, and she never went out on her own anyway. Why would she?

She was going to tell Steve to leave her alone and she knew she would have to do it soon.

Rosalind was under no illusions as to what lay behind her problems. She and Mike had been trying for a baby on and off for ages, There was nothing wrong with either of them and they had been for all the tests and tried all the usual medical things, including IVF, but it made no difference.

Something was stopping them starting a family.

Then recently it seemed Mike had lost interest in her altogether and she was feeling rather unloved.

Rosalind wanted the typical family and they had worked out that even just on Mike's salary, they could fairly comfortably afford the typical modest family house. That was how she met Steve.

She went into the estate agent's offices when she saw a picture of a really nice little house in the window, just to find out a bit more about it, and somehow Steve had got her to put her name on their mailing list.

When the property details started arriving, Mike had gone ballistic. She should have talked to him about it, of course she should; but this rolling unhappy row got in the way. What a mess!

The flat was a mess, too.

After she was made redundant, she had no excuse not to keep their home immaculate.

She stirred herself and went to wash out her coffee cup. She was usually so house proud and almost obsessive about keeping it all clean and tidy, but since this silly row started she knew she had let it slide.

Rosalind sank back down on the sofa and cried.

-o0o-

As he was coming out of the offices of Oakshott, Parslow & Partners, Solicitors and Commissioners for Oaths, Geoffrey held the door open for Sylvia Pendle, who was on her way in.

On Mr. Brownlow's recommendation, Sylvia had come to instruct these solicitors in the matter of the sale of her house, and had an appointment to see their Mrs Pauline Patrick, who was to act on her behalf.

Sylvia did not know it of course, but Mrs Patrick had recently been promoted to the position as Head of Conveyancing, on the retirement of old Mr. Shotter, who had held the post for over twenty years.

Mrs Patrick had been with Oakshott, Parslow & Partners, for fifteen of those years, just waiting and hoping for this moment and, now that it had arrived, she had decided to make some sweeping changes to modernise the conveyancing department from the ground up.

She had started by offering the post of 'Trainee Paralegal' to Dawn DeSantos, who left school at the same time as Martin Dartnell-Parkes, although Dawn did have an 'A' level and several more GCSEs than Martin could boast.

Oakshott, Parslow & Partners, had snapped her up as the most promising of what, it must be said, was a pretty ordinary bunch of school leavers this year.

Dawn was a decorative girl, with rather lovely fingernails which she filed almost continuously as she sat at the smaller of the two desks in the outer office of the Conveyancing Department, waiting for something to happen.

When Mr. Shotter retired, Helen, the department's secretary resigned and went to work at Waitrose. Until a replacement was found, Dawn DeSantos was expected, amongst her other duties (such as they were) to meet and greet visitors to the department and show them through to Mrs Patrick's office.

Dawn knew Sylvia Pendle from school, of course, and had attended her 'literature appreciation' sessions in the library in her last two terms there, so she was able to greet her warmly.

The Conveyancing Department, it has to be said, had not been especially busy for the last few months and old Mr. Shotter's attempts to drum up business had not been a great success. As a result, the firm had had to let the other conveyancing clerk go, and the full weight and burden of the entire portfolio of work now fell just to Mrs Patrick, with assistance from Dawn DeSantos when she was not on one of her two days a week at college training to be a Paralegal.

That said, apart from the need to appoint a secretary/receptionist, the department was not what one might call understaffed. The burden of existing cases could best be described as 'light' and Mrs Patrick had been delighted to be able to offer her services to Ms. Sylvia Pendle, in the matter of the sale of her house.

While Dawn made the tea, Mrs Patrick cleared her desk and opened discussions, as she always did with a new client, by explaining the fees payable.

-oOo-

Bryn Williams might have been the only painter she had ever met who had actually managed to sell any of his paintings, but regardless of any monetary value they may have, Sylvia Pendle hated them all.

Now she had a hammer.

===========================

To read more of 'Double Life Insurance' and Bob Able's other books go to Amazon and search 'Bob Able books'.

You can take a look at the rest of Bob Able's books by entering Bob Able Books on Amazon where you will find the full collection. Please leave a review if you enjoyed this book.

Disclaimer:

Note: All rights reserved. No part of this book, ebook or manuscript or associated published or unpublished works may be copied, reproduced or transmitted by any means, electronic, mechanical, photocopying or otherwise, without the prior written permission of the author.

Copyright: Bob Able 2024

The author asserts the moral right under the Copyright, Design and Patents Act 1988 to be identified as the author of this work.

This is a work of fiction, Any similarities between any persons, living or dead and the characters in this work is purely co-incidental.
The author accepts no claims in relation to this work.

Acknowledgements:
With thanks to Philip Wood for his help editing this book and to Jennifer Longhurst for spending such a lot of time to get this right.

Photo credits (cover):
'Blackieshoot' - mushrooms.
Patrick Kalkman - rat.

Carl Gelin - dining room.
Kejetan Sumila - wine.
Irene Bersani - Whitehall

About the author:

Bob Able is a bestselling writer of popular memoirs, fiction and thrillers. He describes himself as a 'part time ex-pat' splitting his time between his homes in coastal Spain and 'darkest Norfolk' in the UK.

His memoir **'Spain Tomorrow'** was rated as the **third most popular travel book** by Amazon in September 2020 and continues to top the charts. With the sequel 'More Spain Tomorrow', these charming lighthearted insights into his life continue to amuse readers.

All his books are available as ebooks and paperbacks and can be found by entering 'Bob Able' in the search bar.

If you like Bob Able's distinctive writing style and would like to read more of his work, here is a little more information.....

Bob Able writes with a lighthearted touch and does not use graphic descriptions of sex or violence in his books, that is not his style. He prefers to leave that sort of thing to the reader's imagination.

He has also produced a new series of lighthearted thrillers which will amuse as well as captivate readers. They are ideal 'beach reads' to take on holiday. The **Bobby Bassington Stories** include:
'Bobbie And The Spanish Chap',
'Bobbie And The Crime-Fighting Auntie',
'Bobbie And The Wine Trouble'
And **'Auntie Caroline's Last Case'**

All these books can be read on their own, although if you read them as a series, 'Auntie Caroline's Last Case' draws all the strings together and completes the tales of the lives of all the characters we meet along the way.

Early reviewers had suggested that these stories would make an engaging TV series and of course Bob would be pleased to hear from television companies and promoters to explore that option!

His fictional novels include **'Double Life Insurance'** a fast moving but lighthearted thriller, where Bobbie Bassington first makes an appearance, fresh out of university, **'No Point Running'** which is set in the world of horse racing in the 1970's, **'The Menace Of Blood'**, which is about inheritance, not gore, and the sequel **'No Legacy of Blood'**. They are engaging thrillers, with a touch of romance and still with that gentle, signature Bob Able humour.

His semi-fictional memoir **'Silke The Cat, My Story'**, written with his friend and wine merchant, Graham Austin and Silke the Cat herself, is completely different. Silke is a real cat, she lives today in the Costa Blanca, and her adventures, which she recounts in this amusing book, really happened (also available as an audio book).

Contact:

bobable693@gmail.com

This is a 'live email address' and is monitored by Bob himself, so do not expect automated replies … Bob hates that sort of impersonal thing.

You can find details of how to buy all Bob's books and also follow him at:

www.amazon.com/author/bobable

Or just enter **'Bob Able books'** on the Amazon site or Google and the full list should appear.

Thank you for reading!

Printed in Great Britain
by Amazon